The COMBAHEE RIVER RAID

The COMBAHEE RIVER RAID

HARRIET TUBMAN & LOWCOUNTRY LIBERATION

JEFF W. GRIGG

THE
History
PRESS

Published by The History Press
Charleston, SC 29403
www.historypress.net

First published 2014

Manufactured in the United States

ISBN 978.1.62619.474.8

Library of Congress CIP data applied for.

To my wife, Barbara, who has always stood by my side.

CONTENTS

ACKNOWLEDGEMENTS

I wish I could say I holed myself up in my office with my computer, my books and papers and simply sat down and wrote this book. But like any other author, I needed help and encouragement—and a lot of it!

I first heard about the Combahee Ferry Raid about twenty-five years ago. To find anything in those days, before the Internet was so prevalent, meant a trip to a library or lengthy correspondence with someone who might have a bit of information.

About fifteen years ago, the South Carolina Department of Transportation decided to widen U.S. Highway 17 and the bridge over the Combahee River about seven miles from my home. Being that it was in the formative stages of the project, the department had little idea of the historical significance of the area, particularly the bridge and causeway. This caused me to write papers, feed information to newspapers and hold meetings to inform them of the historical importance of the area. While I worked in this endeavor, some historians and friends involved in historic preservation encouraged me to put what I had to paper. So began this book.

One of the first to encourage me was Dr. Stephen R. Wise, noted author, historian and director at the Parris Island Museum. Dr. Wise opened his library and research to me at the museum. Each time he or I would find some little scrap on the raid, we would immediately e-mail or phone the other.

A good friend, Cynthia Porcher, pushed me hard as well. Her interest in women's studies, Harriet Tubman and the Gullah people gave me another perspective. She was also generous in opening her research materials to me.

Valerie Marcil, formerly with the South Carolina State Historic Preservation Office, backed me up in my battles with the DOT over a road-widening project at the site of Combahee Ferry and provided with me material from the South Carolina Archives.

Ms. Gary Brightwell of the Colleton County Museum and Dr. Sarah Miller of the Colleton County Historical and Preservation Society both encouraged my work and gave me opportunities to share it in presentations. Gary was also there years earlier in the Colleton County Memorial Library reference room, making sure I had what I needed.

My good friend Bill Olendorf, fellow "Trench Nerd," spent countless hours in the field walking over the very land on which the raid took place. I can still hear him calling out for the snakes to move away. He didn't care that they are deaf.

At the National Park Service in Washington is a very unassuming man, a historian, who works from a government-issued cubicle. David Lowe, an author in his own right, is the spiritual leader of the "Trench Nerds." We're a group that, for fun, goes into the woods to study mounds of old dirt, Civil War earthworks. David invited me to work with him over the course of a week in identifying Civil War cultural resources and mapping them at the Cumberland Gap National Historic Park. During our time together and at numerous other meetings, David reviewed my work in progress, giving suggestions, editing and encouraging—not to mention going on a few trips to the National Archives and the Library of Congress to pick up a reference or two.

Dr. Phil Shiman is a most enthusiastic teacher and friend who spent countless hours schooling me in the structure of old dirt. Phil confirmed the existence of some of the earthworks at Combahee Ferry.

Thanks to Milton Sernett, whom I have never met but have corresponded with, for his wonderful work on Tubman, and Kate Clifford Larson, who has written probably the finest book on Tubman to date. Her wonderful research on the early life of Tubman fills in many gaps and gives us a complete picture. While she and I differ on the wartime experiences of Tubman, her book fulfills a need in Tubman research.

Congressman James Clyburn showed interest in saving earthworks at Combahee Ferry, be they Confederate or Federal. Thank you for your support with the road project and saving history.

South Carolina representative Reverend Kenneth Hodges encouraged my work and invited me to speak at the dedication of the Harriet Tubman Memorial Bridge over the Combahee River.

ACKNOWLEDGEMENTS

I have had the unique privilege to visit numerous plantations involved in the raid in order to research, identify and map the existing earthworks and to understand the lay of the land. Most of the owners and managers do not want to be publically identified, but you know who you are. Thank you for preserving our shared history.

Thanks to my commissioning editor, Chad Rhoad, who put up with my delays, rewrites and questions but never gave up on this project.

Finally, thanks to my wife, Barbara, for her patience over these many years and her unending encouragement to complete this book. Without her, it would not have been finished.

Harriet Tubman. *Library of Congress.*

INTRODUCTION

With numerous retellings of the story, the Combahee River Raid has evolved into a military action led by Harriet Tubman in which she was a spy, a scout and a commander. Numerous authors have taken artistic license to extol the exploits of Tubman, conveniently ignoring the facts instead of relying on the supposition of twentieth-century authors and the writings of friends in support of a pension application. While they elevate the mythology of Tubman to fit their narrative, they overlook the actions of the eager but ill-trained black soldiers of the Second South Carolina Volunteers. The military tactics of Montgomery and the philosophy of Hunter in raising the regiment are not widely known. Elevating Tubman's stature to military commander of the raid has eclipsed her more important role as a leader of a group of scouts who gathered vital intelligence for Union army headquarters, which is almost universally ignored. There is little in the way of direct documentary sources regarding her wartime activities. Many claims made about her were never acknowledged or described by Tubman herself. So, we are left to piece together her story from the few sources we have.

The raid's origins date back to the 1850s and the troubles in Kansas, where, due to the Kansas-Nebraska Act, pro- and antislavery forces went head to head in violent conflict. Out of this maelstrom came men like John Brown, who sought to instigate a slave rebellion, and James Montgomery, a man who shared Brown's abolitionist passion. With a civil war looming on the horizon, Colonel David Hunter, a West Point officer, was drawn into the conflict, during which he interacted with Montgomery as his commander and formulated his abolitionist philosophy—a philosophy forged as much from a desire of command and to ingratiate himself to those he perceived were in a position to further his career. This made him Montgomery's natural ally when war moved from the frontier into South Carolina.

On the other side of the country, a small black woman quietly (for the most part) went about her work rescuing family and friends from bondage in Maryland. Harriet Tubman turned her militancy into a cause, rescuing more than seventy people. It was due to her work using the Underground Railroad that she, too, was introduced to the abolitionist movement and its prominent members, including John Brown of Kansas, who counted James Montgomery as one of his men.

In 1863, General David Hunter, Colonel James Montgomery and Harriet Tubman all played roles in a coastal South Carolina raid that not only freed almost eight hundred men, women and children but also brought a new form of warfare to the Civil War—a brand of scorched-earth warfare that would soon become all too commonplace in the Deep South and lead to General William Tecumseh Sherman's policy of taking the fight to the civilian populace.

The Combahee action caused an uproar in the South and caused the wholesale removal of slaves from the coastal areas, where they were vulnerable to Union raids, to plantations farther inland, leaving the breadbasket of South Carolina barren in fallow fields. At the same time, the Combahee River Raid proved the usefulness and bravery of the black soldier.

Harriet Tubman is one of this nation's greatest heroes and deserving of the accolades bestowed on her. But accolades should be bestowed for her rightful place in history, not for a story based on hearsay and conjecture. At the same time, James Montgomery and David Hunter also deserve acknowledgement for what they did for the abolitionist cause and the integration of black Americans into the United States armed forces.

CHAPTER I

THEY CALLED HER MOSES

She was known by many names during her life. As a child, she was "Minty." John Brown referred to her as "General." The slaves called her "Moses." But no matter how she was known, she was a woman of deep convictions, extraordinary wisdom and courage. She was Harriet Tubman.[1]

The earliest accounts of Harriet's early life were revealed in 1863 in the *Commonwealth*, a Boston newspaper edited by Franklin B. Sanborn, a fervent abolitionist from New England who would become one of her greatest supporters. According to the *Commonwealth*, Tubman was born sometime in 1820 or 1821. In her book *Bound for the Promised Land*, Kate Clifford Larson makes note of a midwife receipt that dates her birth to 1822.[2]

Born Araminta Ross, "Minty," as she was known, was the child of Harriet "Rit" Green and Ben Ross. Minty was initially raised on the Anthony Thompson farm in Dorchester County, on the Eastern Shore of Maryland.[3]

Minty had seven siblings: Linah, born 1808; Mariah, 1811; Soph, 1813; Robert, 1816; Ben, 1823, Henry, 1839; and Moses, 1832. A couple years later, the family was torn apart when Rit's owner, Edward Brodess, took her and her children to his farm near Bucktown, leaving Ben Ross with Thompson.[4] Three of Minty's sisters—Soph, Mariah and Linah—were sold by Brodess. When Brodess tried to sell her brother Moses, the youngest child, to a slave trader, Rit, with the help of free blacks in the community, hid him in the woods for a month. Rit resisted all efforts to turn over her son to Brodess and the slave trader. Brodess eventually abandoned the sale of Moses, leaving him on the farm. The resistance of Rit in the sale of her son contributed to Minty's belief in the resistance to slavery. Her strong bond to her relations and this fracturing of the family must have had a great deal to do with her later trips on the Underground Railroad.[5]

Minty was occasionally hired out to temporary masters by Brodess. Her master had too many mouths to feed for a farm of his size. By hiring out his slaves, he relieved himself of the need to feed and clothe them and also made additional money on the side, which he used to increase the size of his farm. Within the system of chattel slavery, slaves were no more than property to be bought, sold and rented.[6]

At the age of six or seven, Minty was hired out to James Cook, the owner of a small nearby farm, to learn the art of weaving, which she refused to do. Cook and his wife were harsh masters, and Minty endured many beatings. At one point in the winter, while ill with the measles, she was sent into the swamps to check the muskrat traps. She was sent back to her mother, who nursed her back to health, only to see her returned back to the Cooks.[7]

After serving the Cooks, Minty was hired out to a young married woman, a "Miss Susan." Here she endured daily beatings for the smallest of infractions. Minty was charged with taking care of Miss Susan's child, often staying up all night to rock him when sick. If she fell asleep or the child cried, a whip would be brought down on Minty's face, neck or shoulders—scars she carried with her for the rest of her life.[8]

Life with other temporary masters was no better. As she was someone else's property, the temporary masters cared little about the well-being of the young girl in their charge. On one occasion, she refused to be whipped by her mistress. When the master of the house arrived home, he sent Minty upstairs to do some menial task. While she was engaged in this, he came up behind her and beat her savagely, breaking her ribs in the process. Unable to work from the beating, she was sent home to the Brodresses and the care of her mother.[9]

As a teenager, while trying to intervene between an overseer and a slave, Minty was hit in the head by a two-pound weight thrown by the overseer. Bleeding profusely from her wound, she was carried inside with her skull fractured and partially caved in. Receiving only the care of her fellow slaves, she eventually recovered but was left with fainting spells and bouts of severe headaches for the rest of her life.[10]

Once again, Minty was returned to the Brodesses as damaged goods. Brodess tried to sell her, to no avail, as no one wanted to buy a slave unable to work.

Eventually, Minty recovered and worked for five or six years for John T. Stewart, where she also ended up working alongside and probably living with her father. This also brought her closer to her mother and other members of her family. By 1840, her father, Ben Ross, had been manumitted by a provision in the will of his former master, Anthony Thompson. So while Ben was now free, Rit and her children were still in bondage.[11]

In 1844, Minty Ross married free black John Tubman and took on the name Harriet, most likely in honor of her mother. They had no children. While John Tubman was somewhat vilified in later stories told by Harriet, Kate Larson argued that it took a lot for John to marry Harriet. She was still a slave and subject to the desires of her master. In addition, any children she would have borne him would also be enslaved—not a matter to be taken lightly by a free black.[12]

It was during this period of her life that Harriet took to hiring herself out to different masters to do a variety of work. Brodess found this a good way to relieve himself of the burden of trying to hire out "damaged goods" and to bring in a steady income. Harriet's fee to Brodess was guaranteed by Dr. Anthony Thompson, who paid Brodess. Harriet then paid Thompson and was free to keep any additional money she earned. With the additional money, she bought oxen and used them to haul timber from the forests, making her a more valuable hire.[13]

During her middle years, Harriet worked a variety of jobs in the community, including farming, hauling timber and working the stock in Stewart's store. She was known as a strong and hard worker, despite her bouts of fainting. Working the store and the wharfs brought Tubman into direct contact with a large group of both freed blacks and slaves. Many of these men were mariners, hired to transport goods to ports farther up the coast. Being free, they were able to mingle with people in both black and white communities, particularly those in the abolitionist movement and those who aided escaping slaves. Information about escape routes and contacts would have been available to one who was actively seeking it.[14]

With the death of Edward Brodess in 1849, Tubman feared the further breakup of the family. Eliza Brodess sought to sell some of the family's slaves but was stymied by stipulations in the will. In his will, Edward had left the bulk of his assets to his wife—but not his slaves, who remained the property of his estate. He left them for her to use, but she did not own them. Eliza petitioned the courts to sell some of the slaves to pay off her many debts, but to no avail. For the moment, Harriett and her family members remained together.[15]

In the late 1840s, Harriet hired a lawyer to research the will of her mother's first owner, Atthow Pattison. The attorney determined that her mother, Rit, had been manumitted in his will to be freed when she reached the age of forty-five. Edward Brodess had ignored the will, keeping Rit in bondage and thus illegally selling two of her daughters and profiting from the sales. This resulted in a number of legal challenges to Brodess's ownership and the right of Eliza to sell some of the slaves to pay debts. Eliza petitioned the court to sell Kessiah, Harriet's niece. Hearing of the rumors, Harriet decided that it was now time to make her escape. Convincing her two brothers, Ben and Henry, to go with her, they left for the North.[16] However, they shortly returned on their own, bringing Harriet back with them. A few weeks later, Tubman made good on her escape once again, this time making her way to freedom in Philadelphia.[17] Tubman later recounted crossing the Pennsylvania line, "When I found I had crossed that line, I looked at my hands to see if I was the same person. There was such a glory over everything; the sun came like gold through the trees, and over the fields, and I felt like I was in Heaven."[18]

Tubman, using connections in the free black community, aided in the escape of her niece Kessiah and her two children. Kessiah was scheduled to be sold at public auction to the highest bidder. At the auction, held on the courthouse steps, a high bid of $500 was made. But as it turned out, it was a false bid by Kessiah's husband, John Bowley. Before the ruse was uncovered, Bowley had secreted away Kessiah and her children. They traveled to Baltimore, where they met Tubman and were then taken to Philadelphia.[19]

Tubman returned to Baltimore to aid in the escape of her brother Moses and two other men shortly after Kessiah's escape.[20]

With these successes, Tubman decided to return to her former home and bring her husband back with her up North. Making her way to Dorchester County, she sent word to John that she wanted him to go with her. Tubman was devastated to learn that John, in the two years since she had left, had taken another wife, a free black woman, and refused to go. She was furious at John for turning his back on her, but she soon got over the heartbreak. Harriet didn't leave Maryland empty-handed, however, as she guided a small group of slaves to Philadelphia.[21]

With the passage of the Fugitive Slave Act in 1850, slaves who had escaped to the North were no longer considered free. This federal law forced Northerners to assist Southern slave owners or bounty hunters in their efforts to recapture escaped slaves. Consequently, the United States was no longer a safe haven. Kessiah and John Bowley and their family headed for Canada.[22]

In December 1851, Tubman escorted a group of eleven escapees to Canada, stopping at the home of Fredrick Douglass. Douglass, an escaped slave himself, was one of the leaders of the abolitionist movement. He might have known Tubman from his days as a slave in Maryland, or they might have simply had any number of close friends and family ties. They had many close ties in the Eastern Shore area. Douglass probably helped spread the story of Tubman among his friends and supporters in the North, helping Tubman enlarge her circle of contacts and giving her more legitimacy in her efforts.[23]

Word got to Harriet that her three brothers—Henry, Ben and Robert—were to be put on the auction block by Eliza Brodess the day after Christmas 1854. Accordingly, Harriet quickly made plans to get to them through intermediaries. Robert had a dilemma, however: his wife, Mary, was pregnant and about to give birth. If Robert left now, he would be leaving his wife, two young sons and infant daughter. If he didn't leave, he would probably be sold and moved to the Deep South, never to see his family again. While Mary was initially unaware of his plans, Robert finally confessed to her his desire to escape. Seeing no other option, Mary finally relented and gave him her blessing. Robert hurried to meet his brothers and sister.[24]

Harriet, her brothers and three others—including Ben's fiancée, Jane—made their way north. Traveling at night and hiding during the day, they covered the one hundred miles to Philadelphia in four days, arriving in the city on December 29.[25]

Tubman made numerous trips back to Maryland, seeking the freedom of the rest of her family. In 1857, she brought out her aged parents, both of whom were over seventy. The mood of the slaveholders on the Eastern Shore grew increasingly militant as their slaves dared to try to escape, at times as many as fifteen from a single plantation. The free black community came under closer scrutiny, and some were arrested. Harriet sometimes spent months in the area, looking for the right opportunity to help her family and friends to escape. After guiding her parents to Canada, the Eastern Shore became too dangerous even for Tubman. That, coupled with the financial and physical hardships she endured, brought an end to her trips down south. However, by this time, Harriet Tubman was known and respected widely by those on the Underground Railroad and in abolitionist circles.[26]

Interestingly, in Sarah Bradford's 1869 biography *Scenes in the Life of Harriet Tubman*, she records Tubman as having made nineteen trips to the South, during which she rescued three hundred slaves. Conrad, in his book *Harriet Tubman*, cites various numbers and can't seem to come to a conclusion. Larson states that Tubman made thirteen trips and brought out about seventy to eighty people, a much more believable number. Although according to

Larson, Harriet herself claimed only eight or nine trips and fifty people.[27] Regardless of the exact number of trips of enslaved individuals brought to freedom in the less than ten years she led those out of bondage, Tubman was one of the most prolific conductors on the Underground Railroad.

Tubman soon found herself recognized and lauded by the leading abolitionist figures of the day, including Fredrick Douglass, Franklin Sanborn, William H. Seward, William Still, Thomas Wentworth Higginson and even John Brown. It was John Brown himself who probably gave Tubman the nickname "General."[28] To note the occasion of Tubman's death the previous day, the March 11, 1913 *Auburn Citizen* newspaper printed the following account of Brown introducing her to a friend:

> *A letter written by Wendell Phillips to an Auburn lady in June 16, 1868, says regarding Harriet Tubman: "The last time I ever saw John Brown was under my roof when he brought Harriet Tubman to me, saying, 'Mr. Phillips, I bring you one of the best and bravest persons on this continent—General Tubman, as we call her.'" The famous leader of Ossawatomie, narrating to Boston's famous preacher, the career of Harriet and concluding for himself, said: "In my opinion there are few captains, perhaps few colonels, who have done more for the colored race than our fearless and sagacious friend, Harriet."[29]*

John Brown had formulated an idea of leading a slave revolt, an uprising through the South culminating in a free state for the blacks in western Maryland and Virginia. His plans were to attack the U.S. arsenal at Harpers Ferry, Virginia; supply the slaves and his supporters with arms from the arsenal; and lead the revolt. Brown thought that the only way to end slavery was by force, and he fully expected that the enslaved people of the South would rise up with him against their masters, throwing off the chains of bondage.[30]

Brown solicited the help of some prominent abolitionists of the day, who agreed to financially and materially support Brown and his plan. Known as the Secret Six, these prominent Bostonians were: Franklin B. Sanborn, George L. Sterns, Thomas Wentworth Higginson, Theodore Parker, Samuel G. Howe and Gerrit Smith.[31]

Tubman was living in Canada at the time John Brown was planning the raid on Harpers Ferry. In April 1858, Brown traveled to Canada to meet with the woman he had heard so much about. He solicited her help in recruiting freed slaves living in Canada to assist in the raid. Tubman held a meeting at her home and invited a few of the former slaves she had helped out of bondage. Here, Brown was able to recruit a number of the men to aid in the insurrection. Tubman became an ardent supporter and admirer of Brown. She sought more recruits to aid Brown in the insurrection. On May 8, Brown held what became known as the Chatham Convention to reveal his plans and sign up recruits. Tubman did not attend, nor did his Massachusetts supporters.[32]

After Brown's convention, word of his plans were leaked by Hugh Forbes to Massachusetts senator Henry Wilson. Afraid of being exposed, the Secret Six met with Brown and decided to delay the raid. Brown simply didn't have the resources to conduct the raid, and he reluctantly returned to Kansas.[33]

In late 1858, Tubman went to Boston to raise funds for the black community in Canada. There, she met Franklin B. Sanborn. Sanborn, a confidant of John Brown and one of the Secret Six, was well regarded in the abolitionist movement. He became one of Tubman's close friends and greatest supporters and later wrote one of the first biographies of Tubman.[34]

Tubman also met and became friends with Senator William H. Seward, who owned a piece of property in Auburn, New York, which he sold to Tubman on very favorable terms. The property was enough for Tubman to move her aged parents and any other family members who wished to accompany them out of the harsh Canadian climate and back to the United States.[35]

In order to help pay for the property, Harriet once again returned to Boston and made the rounds of the supporters of the abolitionist movement, telling tales of her many trips to the Eastern Shore. Harriet soon saw the financial rewards of telling her story and realized that her remarkable life could be financially rewarding. While in Boston, she met with John Brown, who had also returned to the city to raise money for his planned raid. It was in Boston that Brown and Tubman planned their next moves.[36]

It is unknown exactly why Tubman didn't go on the raid with Brown. The generally recognized excuse is that she was ill at the time. Others speculate that she had finally seen the futility of the raid. But whatever the reason, Tubman didn't go, saving herself a trip to the gallows with Brown and his men. While Brown's raid failed in terms that it did not incite a slave revolt, it did galvanize the South against Northern interests, further dividing the nation. Brown became a martyr to the abolitionist cause and a rallying point for years to come, inspiring Federal soldiers in recruitment and song.

In April 1861, Confederate batteries in Charleston, South Carolina, fired on the Federal garrison stationed at Fort Sumter, bringing about the start of the Civil War. This brought a permanent end to any thoughts Harriet had of returning to Maryland and helping anyone else escape. Recruits rushed to enlist on both sides, and the ranks of both armies swelled. Tubman during this time tended to matters back in Auburn, occasionally visiting some abolitionist friends.

Lincoln, his cabinet and his generals formulated plans for the coming war. General Winfield Scott, commanding general of the Federal forces, proposed the Anaconda Plan, whereby the U.S. Navy would blockade the Southern ports, choking them off from supplies and materials from foreign nations. The Federals needed a port of operations, and Port Royal, being one of the finest harbors in the South and with a relatively small population, would make a perfect base of operations to supply the naval ships. Accordingly, in November 1861, the U.S. Navy sailed into Port Royal Sound and immediately drove the defending Confederates from Forts Walker and Beauregard. With the fall of the forts on the Sea Islands, the plantation owners fled, leaving most of their possessions behind, including thousands of slaves.[37] The following day, Federals moved into Beaufort, where they found that the escaped slaves, or "contrabands," were in possession of the town.

May 1862 brought Harriet Tubman to Port Royal.

At the request of Governor John Andrew of Massachusetts, Harriet was sent south to aid the thousands of contrabands abandoned on the Sea Islands and making their way from the mainland. Tubman and many others traveled by steamer to Beaufort and Hilton Head, where they went to work helping to settle and teach the newly freed slaves.[38]

Upon reaching Beaufort, Tubman first worked at the Christian Commission, handing out supplies, food and clothing to the Union soldiers. She then established a "washhouse" with $200 she had received from the government. The washhouse was where she taught the former slaves how to sew, wash for the soldiers and make baked goods—the idea being to turn the slave-based economy into a wage-based economy for the blacks. On returning from one trip to Florida, she found that her washhouse had been destroyed by some newly arrived troops. Harriet was never compensated for her loss.[39]

Harriet made baked goods and root beer in order to support herself and earn some much-needed money to send home to Auburn. General Hunter aided her in this by allowing Harriet to purchase needed supplies from the army commissary.[40]

General David Hunter
February 19, 1863

Pass the bearer, Harriet Tubman, to Beaufort, and back to this place, and wherever she wishes to go, and give her passage at all times on all Government transports. Harriet was sent to me from Boston, by Gov. Andrew, of Mass., and is a valuable woman. She has permission, as a warrant of the Government, to purchase such provisions from the commissary as she may need.[41]

The climate in the Department of the South was unhealthy in the summer, and many of the soldiers fell ill from the prevalent diseases. Tubman assisted the Union surgeons in the hospitals. As wounded soldiers were brought back to the area from engagements in Florida and up and down the South Carolina coast, she took to working with them as well. Tubman worked the hospitals all day and into the night and then returned home to make her pies and root beer.[42]

Tubman explained how she bathed and dressed the wounds of the soldiers: "I'd go to the hospital, I would, every morning. I'd get a big chunk of ice, I would, and put it in a basin, and fill it with water. Then I'd take a sponge and begin…by the time I had bathed off three or four the heat and fire would have melted the ice and made the water warm, and it would be as red as clear blood. Then I would go get some more ice."

During one particularly virulent bout of illness in Florida, Tubman was sent to help nurse the sick troops. Here, Tubman used her extensive knowledge of roots and herbs to alleviate the suffering and cure some of the ailments.[43]

Tubman during this time was in constant contact with the escaping slaves making their way through the Confederate lines to Beaufort, Port Royal Island and Hilton Head. She was also well known by the Union officers, most of whom, like General David Hunter, were known for their abolitionist views. This meant that Harriet, unlike other blacks from the area, had close contact and the ear of the officers.

Most slaves who made their way through the lines had little trust in these new white men and refused to answer to Union soldiers. Tubman, on the other hand, was a familiar face, and as they poured through the lines, she would take the time to garner what information she could from them about Confederate dispositions in the interior. Time and again escapees were told that they needed to go see "Miss Harriet."[44]

Tubman seems to have been working with some local scouts as well as some operatives from up north. Some of the men she worked with were locals who were very familiar with the area and more than willing to divulge information to Harriet. Being so familiar with the waterways and plantations, a few returned, risking capture to further gather intelligence of the Confederate troop movements. In her petition for a pension after the war, Harriet said as much, noting that she had been "a commander of several men (eight or nine) as scouts during the late War of the Rebellion, under directions and orders of Edwin M. Stanton, Secretary of War, and of several Generals."[45]

While in Beaufort, Tubman met with an old friend, Thomas Wentworth Higginson. Higginson, the Unitarian minister who, on his lecture tours before the war, often recited many of Tubman's exploits, was now the commander of the First South Carolina Volunteers, the first black regiment formed by General Hunter. A prolific writer, Higginson wrote home about spending some time with Harriet.[46]

In February 1863, Tubman met Colonel James Montgomery, leader of the newly formed Second South Carolina Volunteers. Newly arrived from Kansas by way of Washington, he was one of "John Brown's men." Harriet admired Montgomery's rough, hard attitude toward slave owners and also his religious convictions. In Montgomery, Tubman found someone who actually fought for his convictions and who fought alongside John Brown, putting actions to the forefront. He was a person of action, much like herself.[47]

The stage was set for operations against the coastal rice plantations, settlements and slaveholders.

Chapter 2
JAMES MONTGOMERY

If a man loves God, he will love his brother also. This is the love of God and by
this we know that we love God when we love his brother.
—*James Montgomery*

The 1850s were a turbulent time in Missouri and the Kansas Territory.
With the passage of the Kansas-Nebraska Act in 1854, the Missouri
Compromise, an attempt to regulate slavery and the balance of power in
Congress, was rendered null and void. The new act allowed each territory
or state to regulate slavery within its borders via a doctrine of "popular
sovereignty." Although it was seemingly a more democratic solution, it
resulted in opening the territories to wholesale immigration to boost the
numbers in the territory and to subject the citizens to intimidation and,
eventually, violence.[48]

The brainchild of Senator Stephen Douglass, the act severely damaged
his own Democratic Party, caused the foundering of the Whig Party and
brought the Republican Party to the forefront in the next election cycle.
This splintered the leading parties and made slavery the main issue in the
new lands, upsetting the balance of power in Congress. In effect, it was the
precursor of the next great conflict, the American Civil War.[49]

The act was especially alarming to Missouri, a slave state. While the western
portion of the state along the Missouri border, known as the "black belt,"
was heavily proslavery, the rest of Missouri held very few slaves. If Kansas
were admitted to the Union as a free state, it would tip the congressional

balance in favor of the free states. In addition, as Missouri was surrounded on three sides by free states, this would be an enticement for the slaves within the state to escape to the open prairies of Kansas.[50]

In order to influence the state constitution and whether Kansas would become a free or slave state, thousands of settlers from both sides poured into Kansas. Abolitionists from the New England states paid and sponsored any settlers who would move to Kansas and vote it as a free state. In 1856, a group of approximately thirty proslavery settlers from South Carolina arrived in Bourbon County. They were supposedly sponsored by the Southern Emigrant Aid Society and were members of the Dark Lantern societies. Upon arrival, they terrorized free state settlers and attempted to drive them from the Kansas Territory.[51]

In response to the emigrants from the Northeast and Midwest, thousands of Missourians poured over the border to push their proslavery agenda into the Kansas Territory. In the election to send a delegate to Congress, 1,729 of 2,943 votes were deemed illegal. In the legislative election of March 1855, in a territory of only 2,905 eligible voters, 6,307 votes were cast for the territorial legislature, resulting in 4,908 illegal votes! The majority of the votes were for the proslavery side. The Missourians came heavily armed, intimidated the election officials and then left after having cast their votes.[52] The newly elected territorial legislature was then free to pass laws not only regulating slavery but also limiting the freedoms of those who opposed it. Even though he knew of the rampant fraud, Governor Andrew Reeder initially allowed the election to stand. Reeder later changed his stance, but by that time he had been relieved as governor.[53]

The free state citizens held a convention in September of that same year in response to the fraudulent elections, declaring them null and illegal. They then elected their own legislature and governor. By the spring of 1856, Kansas had two separate governments.[54] The proslavery government, recognized by the Pierce administration, had come as the result of a "stolen election." The government elected by the free state citizens, which was boycotted by the proslavery partisans, was recognized only by the former. Neither side could claim legitimacy. So, the great test of popular sovereignty advocated by Douglas was a failure in its first test.[55]

Violence soon broke out, with Missouri "Border Ruffians" harassing the free state settlers and "enforcing" their proslavery laws. The free state settlers, outraged by the fraudulent election and attacks on their settlements, struck back.

Interestingly, there were never many slaves in Kansas. Even the proslavery settlers from Missouri dared not bring their slaves to Kansas. Those who did settled only in the extreme eastern part of the state.

The Sacking of Lawrence galvanized the Northern view against the proslavery side. Lawrence was an antislavery town formed in 1854 by antislavery settlers, many sent by the New England Emigrant Aid Company. In Lawrence, two newspapers—the *Herald of Freedom* and the *Kansas Free State*—frequently railed against the proslavery view. The Free-State Hotel was the epicenter of the proslavery forces' wrath. A proslavery grand jury found that the hotel had actually been built as a fort and was a "stronghold of resistance to law, thereby endangering public safety."[56] On May 21, 1856, a posse of Southerners led by Douglas County sheriff Samuel Jones laid siege to the hotel and mostly deserted town. When asked to surrender, the remaining defenders did so without a fight. Eventually, they burned the hotel, destroyed the two printing presses and sacked the town.[57]

In response to the Sacking of Lawrence, John Brown, one of the more violent free state men, removed five proslavery settlers from their homes near Pottawatomie Creek and, with his sons, summarily murdered them. At the time, Brown lived in Linn County and was a friend of James Montgomery.[58] This led to outright warfare between the free state settlers and the proslavery forces resulting in murder, the stealing of livestock and the plundering of settlers' homes.

One of the most infamous "jayhawkers" from Kansas was James Montgomery, confidant of John Brown and, later, colonel of the Second South Carolina Volunteers (Union). Montgomery, born in Ohio in 1814, had moved to Kentucky at the age of twenty-three and was employed as a schoolteacher and minister in the Campbellite Church. In the early 1850s, he moved to Polk County, Missouri.[59] With the passage of the Kansas-Nebraska Act of 1854, he moved once again, this time to Linn County, Kansas (which was mostly proslavery at this time), near Mound

James Montgomery. *National Park Service.*

City. Montgomery bought a piece of land from a proslavery settler on Little Sugar Creek.[60]

In 1856, when many free state settlers were being driven off their land, James Montgomery refused to leave. As a reward for his refusing to leave, Montgomery's home was fired on and then burned. Undaunted, Montgomery rebuilt, but this time he built the house as a fortress, complete with a hidden escape tunnel. Instead of leaving in 1857, he formed his own "band" of men to protect the free settlers and runaway slaves in southeast Kansas and also to harass proslavery settlements in both Kansas and Missouri. Montgomery's antislavery feelings turned more radical. On September 16, 1857, Montgomery was appointed "Captain of the Little Sugar Creek Company" by James H. Lane.[61]

Joining forces with John Brown in July 1858, Montgomery soon gained a reputation for plunder and violence. He and his men conducted frequent raids in Missouri, stealing horses and livestock and burning homesteads. In Kansas, Montgomery gave warning to the proslavery settlers to clear out or suffer his wrath, as he would not allow their politics or violence.

December 1858 found Montgomery leading a force of about one hundred men to the proslavery town of Fort Scott. Here, they sought the release of a close confidant of Montgomery's, Benjamin Rice, who Montgomery felt was being illegally held for murder. A gunfight soon ensued between the Free-Soilers and the proslavery residents. During the fight, former sheriff John Little was shot and killed by Montgomery's men. During their retreat from town, some of Montgomery's men participated in plunder and robbery.[62]

In 1859, Montgomery was sought by U.S. marshal William Fain for murder and robbery in Bourbon and Linn Counties. Yet like his friend John Brown, nothing came of it, and he was allowed to go free. Montgomery became a close friend of Brown, and only bad weather prevented him from leading a party to try to free Brown after the raid on Harpers Ferry.[63]

Montgomery was well known in abolitionist circles and made trips back east to consult with some of the leading abolitionists of the day (including Horace Greely and George L. Sterns), attending meetings in New York, Philadelphia and Boston.[64]

Shortly before the start of the Civil War, Montgomery joined with Charles Jennison, another leader of the "Kansas Militia." Together, Montgomery and Jennison led raiding parties into Missouri and to proslavery settlements, stealing livestock, plundering valuables and personal property and burning out the inhabitants.[65]

Montgomery was certainly a galvanizing force in Kansas—you either liked his politics and methods or you didn't. There was no room for any ambivalence. Yet at the same time, Montgomery was a complicated man. He never had much money; he did not use what was gained from the raids and plundering of his men to enrich himself. He was a deeply religious man, never without his Bible, and an itinerant minister. To Montgomery, slavery was against the moral teachings of the Bible. Montgomery was never seen to drink nor, as was so often the custom during battle, utter a cussword. More than anything, Montgomery displayed an air of extreme confidence—confidence in his abilities and in his convictions.[66]

With the firing on Fort Sumter and the "official" start of the Civil War, Montgomery joined the regular army, being elected colonel of the Third Kansas Volunteer Infantry, a part of Senator James H. Lane's "brigade." The Third and Fourth Kansas Volunteers were raised independently of the state government by Senator James Lane, who was commissioned brigadier general by the War Department in Washington, D.C., although he did not formally accept the title, not wanting to give up his Senate seat.[67]

Montgomery took up his old "jayhawking" tactics once again. For lack of formal recognition and incomplete organization, the Third was later consolidated with some other units to form the Tenth Kansas Volunteer Infantry in April 1862.[68] Montgomery remained colonel until December 1862, after a series of disagreements with Senator James Lane and Colonel Charles Jennison over the command of a new unit of black troops. Montgomery then traveled to Washington, where he conferred with some of his old abolitionist friends, as well as Kansas senator Samuel Pomeroy and President Lincoln. After meeting with them, he was authorized to travel to South Carolina, where he, under General David Hunter, formed the Second South Carolina Volunteers, a black regiment.[69]

War Department, Adjutant-General's Office
Washington, January 13, 1863
Col. James Montgomery
Washington, D.C.

SIR: *By direction of the Secretary of War you are hereby authorized to raise, subject to the approval of the general commanding the Department of the South and under his direction, a regiment of South Carolina volunteer infantry, to be recruited in that State, to serve for three years or during the war. The said regiment will be organized as prescribed in General Orders*

No. 126, current series, from this office. All appointments of officers will be made by the War Department. All musters will be made in strict conformity to paragraph 86, Revised Mustering Regulations of 1862.

I am, sir, very respectfully, your obedient servant,

Thomas M. Vincent,
Assistant Adjutant-General

Montgomery brought with him to the South Carolina Lowcountry his own brand of warfare, honed from years on the prairies and in the ravines of Missouri and Kansas.

CHAPTER 3

BLACK DAVE

David Hunter began his military career with his graduation from the U.S. Military Academy in West Point in 1822. Hunter was commissioned a second lieutenant in the Fifth Infantry Regiment. Initially, he was stationed at Fort St. Anthony, Michigan, near what is today St. Paul, Minnesota, an outpost on the far northwestern reaches of the frontier. At Fort St. Anthony, due to his swarthy complexion, Hunter received the nickname "Black Dave," a nickname that would follow him throughout his career.[70]

The second lieutenant was known for being aggressive and not backing down. This caused him to have problems with his commanding officer, Colonel Josiah Snelling. Snelling was fond of challenging his subordinate officers, stating that they could seek personal satisfaction if they disagreed with how he operated. After a number of affronts, Hunter took Snelling up on his offer and challenged him in writing. Instead of accepting the challenge, however, Snelling had Hunter arrested and court-martialed.[71]

After a trial, Hunter was found guilty. However, the court that had recommended his expulsion from the army also recommended clemency from President John Quincy Adams, as it had also found fault with Snelling's conduct. President Adams did, in fact, grant Hunter clemency.[72]

A promotion to first lieutenant followed, along with a reassignment to Fort Dearborn, Illinois (present-day Chicago), in 1828. Hunter married Maria Kinzie, the daughter of a Fort Dearborn fur trader, in September 1832 while on leave from his new post in Green Bay.[73] After serving at a variety of posts on the northwest frontier, Hunter was finally promoted to captain of the new First Dragoons, where he served an additional three years.[74]

In July 1836, Hunter resigned from the army to pursue business interests in real estate in the Illinois area in conjunction with his in-laws. After selling his interest in some Chicago land and turning over his interests in the Lake House hotel to his brother-in-law, Hunter sought to reenter the army.[75] There being no opening for a commander of infantry, he used political patronage to reenter as a paymaster. He was appointed assistant paymaster in November 1841 and transferred to Tallahassee, Florida. By March 1842, he had acquired the rank of major in the regular service and was ordered to Washington.[76]

Major Hunter assumed the duties of paymaster in Arkansas and then, with the outbreak of the war with Mexico, accompanied the U.S forces there. Working strictly as paymaster, Hunter was never given the opportunity to command troops in the conflict.[77]

The year 1856 found Hunter assuming his paymaster duties at a familiar post: Fort Leavenworth, Kansas. At this time, Kansas, as a result of the 1854 Kansas-Nebraska Act, was embroiled in a conflict between proslavery and antislavery settlers known as "Bleeding Kansas." While at Leavenworth, Hunter did little to hide his feelings on the question of slavery and politics. Prior to the 1860 election, Hunter, an outspoken supporter of Lincoln, wrote to the presidential candidate concerned for his safety.[78]

Ft. Leavenworth, Kansas
October 20, 1860

Dear Sir, your success and safety being identified with the great Republican cause, the cause of peace, union and conservatism must be my apology for addressing you. On a recent visit to the east, I met a lady of high character, who had been spending part of the summer among her friends and relatives in Virginia. She informed me that a number of young men in Virginia had bound themselves, by oaths most solemn, to cause your assassination, should you be elected. Now sir, you may laugh at this story, and really it does appear too absurd to repeat, but I beg you to recollect that "on the institution" these good people are most certainly demented and being crazy, they should be taken care of, to prevent their doing harm to themselves or to others. Judicious,

*prompt and energetic action on the part of your Secretary of War will
no doubt secure your own safety and the peace of the country. I have
the honor to be*

Very Sincerely,
David Hunter
U.S. Army

P.S. I had the pleasure of meeting you in early days.[79]

So began a correspondence between Hunter and Lincoln prior to the
election. Hunter wrote again to Lincoln on December 18, 1860, detailing his
fears of a coup on the Lincoln administration. As a result of their friendship
and the confidence Lincoln had in Hunter, he invited Hunter to accompany
him on the train to Washington. Hunter accompanied Lincoln as far as
Buffalo, where he was injured in the crush of a mob wanting to get close to
the president-elect. A few days later, Hunter caught up with Lincoln's train
and rejoined the party.[80]

After Lincoln's inauguration, Hunter was ordered by General Scott, head
of the army, to take charge of the presidential mansion (White House).
Overseeing one hundred men from all parts of the Union, Hunter spent
each night in the East Room for a period of six weeks. Half of the men were
stationed at the mansion, and the other half, commanded by senator-elect
James Lane from the new state of Kansas, stayed at the Willard Hotel across
the street and patrolled the streets at night.[81]

Finally, Hunter received the promotion he always desired: colonel of
the newly formed Sixth Cavalry. Hunter commanded a brigade known
as the "Brigade of the Aqueduct." The regiment was quartered opposite
Georgetown on the Virginia hills.[82]

In June 1861, Hunter was relieved of command of the Sixth Cavalry by
General William T. Sherman and ordered to command the Right Division
of the U.S. Army and advance on Bull Run. At Bull Run, Hunter was
wounded twice, the more serious wound being in the neck. The fifty-eight-
year-old Hunter was forced to relinquish his command.[83]

Two months after Bull Run, Hunter was promoted to major general of
volunteers. With the promotion, Hunter was ordered to report to General
John C. Fremont of the Western Division. Back in familiar territory, Hunter
led the First Division until he was asked to replace General Fremont in
November 1861. Lincoln suggested that his new commander pursue

General David Hunter at the beginning of the war. *Library of Congress.*

Confederate general Sterling Price, but only as far as necessary to secure Missouri and the railheads of the two railroads. In addition, Hunter was to cooperate with Lane, now commander of the Kansas Brigade, on the Kansas border. While just a suggestion, Hunter was more than willing to follow the advice of the president.[84]

Hunter's tenure as commander of the Western Division was short-lived, lasting only a week. Hunter was relieved of command and the division abolished. General George B. McClellan then ordered Hunter to take over the command of the Department of Kansas on November 9, 1861.[85]

After his brief stay in Washington, Kansas senator James Lane secured for himself a commission of colonel from the governor of Indiana. This put him in command of troops he had raised in Kansas. One of Lane's commanders was a familiar face in Kansas, that of James Montgomery. Lane seems to have rejoined the way of the "jayhawkers" when Lane marched his troops north from Fort Scott, supposedly following the Confederates. However, instead of engaging the enemy, Lane plundered and sacked the countryside and burned the town of Osceola, shooting some of the inhabitants in the process.[86]

Fremont had little success in reining in Lane, and so it fell to Hunter to take control of the situation. Hunter found the troops from Kansas in deplorable condition—the men were ill trained, had little or no discipline, and were totally lacking in proper command. He noted that the troops were "in a state of demoralization."[87]

In the meantime, Lane strongly campaigned behind Hunter's back for an expedition from Kansas down to northern Texas. Lincoln was made to believe that Hunter, Lane's commander, had approved the plan. In fact, Hunter was not in favor of the expedition but was ordered to plan it with Lane as his subordinate officer. While Hunter concerned himself with trying to put the new troops in order, Lane found himself in the position of having to give up his senate seat if he took the military commission to lead the expedition. He also found himself in a subordinate position to Hunter and therefore gave up his military commission and chose to remain in the Senate. The days of Lane's jayhawking were over.[88]

Washington, Feb. 10, 1862

My wish has been, and is, to avail the government of the services of both General Hunter and General Lane; and, so far as possible, to personally oblige both. General Hunter is the senior officer, and must command when they serve together; though, in so far as he can, consistently with the public service, and his own honor, oblige General Lane, he will also oblige me. If they cannot come to an amicable understanding, General Lane must report to General Hunter for duty, according to the rules, or decline the service.

A. Lincoln[89]

It was during this time as head of the Department of Kansas that Hunter took to writing Lincoln about his dissatisfaction with the position. Hunter complained that he, a major general, was relegated to a backwater command of 3,000 while a lesser officer, political appointee Brigadier General Don Carlos Buell, was in Kentucky leading a 100,000-man army:

You did me the honor to select me as a Major General, and I am confident you intended I should have a Major General's command. Yet strange as it may appear, I am sent here into banishment, with not three thousand effective men under my command, while one of the Brigadiers, General Buell, is in command of near one hundred thousand men in Kentucky. The only sin I have committed is my carrying out your views in relation to the retrograde movement from Springfield.[90]

Hunter's views on slavery, never really hidden, now came to the forefront. In a letter to Senator Lyman Trumbull, Hunter wrote of his dissatisfaction with his situation and put forth the idea of pushing south if he had Buell's command in Kentucky, "proclaiming the Negro free, and arming him as I go." This was the first time a Union commander had put forth the idea of arming blacks and leading them into combat. Quite possibly, it was due to Hunter's frustration over his situation, or it might have been a way to ingratiate himself with the Radical Republicans and politically better his status.[91]

Shortly, Hunter's Department of Kansas would be gone, too.[92]

CHAPTER 4

DEPARTMENT OF THE SOUTH

GENERAL ORDERS WAR DEPARTMENT
A.G.O. No. 26
March 15, 1862

The States of South Carolina, Georgia, and Florida, with the expedition and forces now under Brig. Gen. T.W. Sherman, will constitute a military department, to be called the Department of the South, to be commanded by Major-General Hunter.

By order of the Secretary of War
L. THOMAS,
Adjutant-General[93]

March 31, 1862, found Hunter with a new command, the Department of the South, composed of the states of South Carolina, Georgia and Florida. Hunter set up his headquarters on Hilton Head, an island off the extreme southern coast of South Carolina.[94]

Just four months earlier, the U.S. Navy had forced its way into Port Royal. The Confederates and the planters fled the Sea Islands and the area surrounding Port Royal and Beaufort. Left behind were the approximately nine thousand newly freed slaves in the immediate coastal area. Brigadier General Thomas W. Sherman was tasked with not only military operations but also coming up with a way to care for the former slaves.[95]

Headquarters of General David Hunter on Hilton Head Island, South Carolina, 1862. *Library of Congress.*

Sherman appealed to the War Department for help, but to little avail. The War Department probably considered the problem of what to do with the ex-slaves a matter for the Treasury Department, which was responsible for collecting taxes from the states in rebellion. To this end, the Treasury Department quickly sought to confiscate any cotton, personal property or anything else of value.[96]

The Treasury Department aimed to put the blacks back to work producing more crops, specifically cotton, from which the government could collect taxes. To accomplish this, it instituted the "Port Royal Experiment," in which the free blacks would be taught and guided to become self-sufficient.[97]

The Treasury Department was to furnish transportation, food and protection for these superintendents, teachers and missionaries. One of the groups called on to help was the Educational Committee for Freedman, which set sail from New York on a government ship, the *Atlantic*, and arrived in Port Royal on March 7, 1862. The group immediately set to work organizing and feeding the blacks, which reduced the strain on the military. Superintendents were placed on each plantation, small plots of land were allotted to each family to raise their own crops and the former slaves were then paid for their labor. The newly freed slaves were not forced to stay on the plantations—in fact, many of the younger men went to work for the government on varying projects as laborers in Beaufort and Hilton Head. The majority of the freedmen and their families, however, did choose to stay on the plantations, where they were familiar with the surroundings.[98]

The fall of Port Royal to the U.S. Navy gave the Federals control of one of the finest ports on the eastern seaboard. It also gave them a base of operations against both Savannah and Charleston, important blockade-running ports. Just south of Port Royal, Savannah was protected by Fort Pulaski, located on a small island near the mouth of the Savannah River. Brigadier General Quincy A. Gilmore engineered the placement of the batteries that would attack the fort. Hunter ordered the Confederates to surrender the fort on April 10. After their refusal, Hunter opened fire, and the fort surrendered within thirty hours. Savannah was no longer a port of entry for the blockade-running Confederates. Now only Charleston, South Carolina, and Wilmington, North Carolina, were left as major ports on the southeast coast.[99]

Hunter was not satisfied with the fall of the fort, however, and he took another step closer to arming the newly freed slaves and incorporating them into the army. Hunter's General Order #7 would apply to Fort Pulaski and the surrounding islands.

General Order No. 7
Hdqrs. Department of the South
April 13, 1862

All persons of color lately held to involuntary service by enemies of the United States in Fort Pulaski and on Cockspur Island, Georgia, are hereby confiscated and declared free, in conformity with law, and shall hereafter receive the fruits of their own labor. Such of said persons of color as are able-bodied and may be required shall be employed in the Quartermaster's department at the rates heretofore established by Brig. T.W. Sherman.

By command of Maj. Gen. D. Hunter[100]

Before leaving Baltimore on his trip to reassume command of the Department of the South in Port Royal, Hunter had asked for additional troops and requested an answer by the time he got to Fort Monroe. When he arrived at Fort Monroe, however, he had not received an answer from Secretary of War Edwin Stanton. Hunter again requested more troops, but again he was ignored. At this time, Hunter thought he was facing sixty-five thousand Confederate troops spread from Charleston to Augusta to Savannah, roughly three times the men he had. In reality, though, he was up against a total of about nineteen thousand Confederates. Shortly after arriving in South Carolina, Hunter asked Stanton for fifty thousand muskets and two hundred rounds of ammunition for each, as well as fifty thousand pairs of scarlet pantaloons in which to arm any "local men" loyal to the Union. It is not known if Hunter had discussed the idea of arming the blacks with Stanton when he was in Washington. But based on Hunter's equipment request, Stanton should have known what he was up to.[101]

Hunter's General Order No. 7 received little notice in the North or in Washington. After all, it applied only to the immediate vicinity of the area around Fort Pulaski. However, the silence from Washington probably emboldened Hunter, as less than a month later, he issued the most sweeping order of emancipation in the war yet, Order No. 11.

General Hunter's Order 11
Hdqrs. Department of the South
Hilton Head, S.C.
May 9, 1862

The three States of Georgia, Florida, and South Carolina, comprising the Military Department of the South, having deliberately declared themselves no longer under the protection of the United States of America, and having taken up arms against the said United States, it becomes a military necessity to declare them under martial law. This was accordingly done on the 25ᵗʰ day of April, 1862. Slavery and martial law in a free country are altogether incompatible. The persons in these three States—Georgia, South Carolina, and Florida—heretofore held as slaves, are therefore declared forever free.

David Hunter
Major-General Commanding[102]

The reaction of President Lincoln was immediate although somewhat subdued. Hunter's Order No. 11 had put the president in a difficult position. He was still courting the border states, not wanting to tip them further toward the Confederacy, and neither the government nor the majority of Northerners were quite ready to emancipate all of the slaves. So, Lincoln issued a draft proclamation.[103]

The initial draft (strikethroughs are Lincoln's) referenced newspaper clippings instead of an "official" proclamation from one of his generals. While many in the North supported Hunter's orders, Lincoln felt he had no choice but to invalidate them, and he further expressed that any such order would come directly from him. Lincoln never sent an official rebuke to Hunter. He later stated, "I valued him nonetheless for his agreeing with me in the general wish that all men everywhere could be free."

I, Abraham Lincoln, president of the United States, proclaim and ~~*declare, that the government of the*~~ *United States, had no knowledge, information, or belief of an intention on the part of General Hunter to issue such a proclamation; nor has it yet, any authentic information that the document is genuine—And further, that neither General Hunter, nor any other commander, or person, has been* ~~*expressly, or implicitly*~~ *authorized by the Government of the United States, to make proclamations declaring the slaves of any state free; and that the supposed proclamation, now in question, whether genuine or false, is altogether void, so far as respects such declaration.*

I further make known that whether it be competent for me, as Commander-in-Chief of the Army and Navy, to declare the slaves of any state or states, free, and whether at any time, in any case, it shall have become a necessity indispensable to the maintenance of the government, to exercise such supposed power, are questions which, under my responsibility, I reserve to myself, and which I ~~*will permit to be decided for me by neither any, nor all of my military subordinates*~~ *cannot feel justified in leaving to the decision of Commanders in the field. These are totally different questions from those of police regulations in armies and camps.*[104]

Prior to Hunter's arrival, orders were given to General T.W. Sherman to guide his employment of the ex-slaves within his department. This order was later used by Hunter to justify some of his actions in raising a regiment. However, he conveniently ignored the sentence concerning the wholesale arming of the blacks (emphasis added).

WAR DEPARTMENT
October 14, 1861
Brigadier General THOMAS W. SHERMAN,
Commanding Expedition to the Southern Coast:

SIR: In conducting military operations within States declared by the proclamation of the President to be in a state of insurrection you will govern yourself, so far as persons held to service under the laws of such States are concerned, by the principles of the letters addressed by me to Major-General Butler on the 30ᵗʰ of May and 8ᵗʰ of August, copies of which are herewith furnished to you. Special directions adapted to special circumstances cannot be given. Much must be referred to your own discretion as commanding general of the expedition. You will, however, in general avail yourself of the services of any persons, whether fugitives from labor or not, who may offer them to the National Government. You will employ such persons in such services as they may be fitted for—either as ordinary employees, or, if special circumstances seem to require it, in any other capacity, with such organization (in squads, companies, or otherwise) as you may deem most beneficial to the service; **this, however, not being a general arming of them for military service.** *You will assure all loyal masters that Congress will provide just compensation to them for the loss of the services of the persons so employed.*[105]

After issuing Order No. 11, Hunter wasted no time in trying to raise a regiment of black troops.

While Hunter was the military commander of the Department of the South, there was a need for a military governor for the area. By early 1862, many of the plantations had superintendents and were back in operation, producing cotton and other crops.

General Saxton's Headquarters, Beaufort, South Carolina. *Library of Congress.*

An 1849 graduate of West Point and a regular officer in the army, Captain Rufus Saxton, now an assistant quartermaster, arrived with the Federal forces in November 1861. A true military man, having graduated from West Point in 1849, Saxton immediately went to work organizing the Federals in the Port Royal area. On March 31, Saxton left his post as quartermaster for Washington. By April 15, 1862, he had been appointed brigadier general of U.S. Volunteers. Before making it back to South Carolina, Saxton was diverted to Harpers Ferry, where he was later awarded the Medal of Honor for defending the town against Stonewall Jackson.[106]

Saxton was charged with the duties of caring for the many plantations, seeing to the welfare of the blacks in the department and raising troops for the black regiments. He and Hunter did not always see eye to eye on the recruitment of blacks.[107]

Washington, D.C.
April 20, 1862
Brig. Gen. R. Saxton

Sir: You are assigned to duty in the Department of the South, to act under the orders of the Secretary of War. You are directed to take possession of all the plantations heretofore occupied by the rebels, and take charge of the inhabitants remaining thereon within the department or which the fortunes of war may hereafter bring into it, with authority to take such measures, make such rules and regulations for the cultivation of the land, and for the protection, employment, and government of the inhabitants, as circumstances may seem to require. The major-general commanding the Department of the South will be instructed to give you all the military aid necessary to enable you to carry out the views of the Government. You will have power to act upon the decisions of courts-martial which are called for the trial of persons not in the military service to the same extent that the commander of a department has over courts-martial called for the trial of soldiers in his department, and so far as the persons above described are concerned, you will also have a general control over the actions of the provost-marshals. It is expressly understood that so far as the persons and purposes herein specified are concerned, your action will be independent of that of the military authorities of the department and in all the cases subordinate only to the major-general commanding. In cases of actual suffering and destitution of the inhabitants, you are directed to issue such portion of the army ration and such articles of clothing as may be suitable to the habits and wants of the persons supplied, which articles will be furnished by the quartermaster and commissary of the Department of the South upon requisitions approved by yourself. It is expected that by encouraging industry, skill in the cultivation of the necessaries of life, and general self-improvement, you will, so far as possible, promote the real well-being of all people under your supervision.

Medical and ordnance supplies will be furnished by the proper officers, which you will distribute and use according to your instructions.

Yours, very truly,

Edwin M. Stanton,
Secretary of War.

P.S.—Report frequently, once a week at least.

Saxton took over the civilian and military affairs as they related to the contraband and the plantations. While not formally a "military governor," he was fulfilling that role.

With the widespread dissemination of Order No. 11, Hunter expected to be able to easily raise the first regiment of blacks. He ordered his commanders to sign up anyone willing to serve and to treat them as they would any other troops. To Hunter's dismay, very few men actually came forward to join the new regiments. Hunter had seriously underestimated the blacks on the plantations, most of whom were more concerned with making new lives for themselves and their families. They chose to stay on the plantations amid familiar surroundings. Additionally, there was a widespread belief and distrust of whites, whom the blacks feared would sell them to Cuba.[108]

The low numbers of willing recruits (on one island, only one man volunteered) caused Hunter to seek more drastic measures to fill the ranks of his black regiments. On May 11, "Black Day," as it was called by some of the teachers on the plantations, Hunter ordered the agents and superintendents of the plantations to send all able-bodied black males from the ages of eighteen to forty-five to Hilton Head. As a consequence, five hundred men were sent from the Sea Islands and Beaufort to Hilton Head, although some escaped to the woods and hid from the agents and soldiers sent to take them.[109]

In a letter, one of the teachers on a nearby plantation summed up the feelings of many of the freedmen: "We made as light of the whole thing as we could, but did not dare to say anything…for the thing they dread is being made to fight, and we knew that there had been men about trying to recruit for Hunter's pet idea, a regiment of blacks."[110]

Those not wanting to remain or not desirable were allowed to return home. Out of this core group, Hunter was able to recruit enough men to start the regiment.

HEADQUARTERS, DEPARTMENT OF THE SOUTH
Hilton Head, S.C.
May 8, 1862.

General ISAAC I. STEVENS,
Commanding, Beaufort, Port Royal Island, &c.:

GENERAL: I am authorized by the War Department to form the negroes into "squads, companies, or otherwise," as I may deem most beneficial to the public service. I have concluded to enlist two regiments to be officered from the most intelligent and energetic of our noncommissioned officers; men who will go into it with all their hearts. If you have any such, please appoint them to officer all the companies you can furnish me except the first. For the first company to be raised at Beaufort I have appointed Captain Trowbridge and two lieutenants from the Volunteer Engineer Regiment. Captain Trowbridge has orders to report to you, and you will very much oblige me if you will furnish him with a good company as soon as possible, and then send him down to report to me. And send, also, other companies as fast as you can have them organized. The noncommissioned officers appointed as officers will not be dropped from the rolls of their respective companies till their new appointments shall have been approved by the President.

Very respectfully, your most obedient servant,

DAVID HUNTER,
Major-General, Commanding

The men who volunteered for the regiment were clothed in red pantaloons and blue coats, armed with muskets and began drilling and training. The regiment formed was the First South Carolina Volunteer Infantry (African Descent).

The news quickly reached Washington that Hunter had indeed raised a regiment of blacks. The reactions of some in Congress were especially strong. Congressman Charles Wickliffe of Kentucky questioned the raising of the regiment and put forth a congressional resolution. Wickliffe specifically asked if the regiment was composed of fugitive or captured slaves and if they had been given any government equipment or arms. Just as Lincoln had done with Order No. 11, Secretary of War Stanton was forced to answer the question. Stanton answered that the War Department had no official knowledge of Hunter raising a regiment but stated that he had asked Hunter for information. However, Stanton did know of the regiment and had, in fact, sent the clothing and arms requested by Hunter, having approved of the plan without Lincoln's knowledge. When asked for any correspondence between the War Department and Hunter, Stanton answered that the president would decline, as the information would not be in the "public's interest."[111]

Hunter, however, took delight in answering Congress, as it brought to a head what he had been trying to accomplish since his days in the Department of Kansas: arming the blacks and incorporating them into the army.[112] On the surface, the questions passed on to Hunter seemed rather simple. Was Hunter authorized to raise a regiment of fugitive slaves and then clothe and arm them?

Hunter answered point by point. First, he stated that "no regiment of fugitive slaves has been or is being organized in this department. There is, however, a fine regiment of persons whose late masters are fugitive rebels." Clearly, Hunter was declaring the men freedmen and not fugitives or slaves. Secondly, Hunter replied that General T.W. Sherman had "distinctly authorized me to employ all loyal persons offering their services in defense of the Union and for the suppression of this rebellion in any manner I might see fit." Finally, regarding the question of arming the regiment, Hunter stated he had not been given any direct orders as to the dispensation of the arms, nor had he been given orders as to the use of hand tools such as shovels given to common laborers.[113]

As the letter was read to the assembled House, "peals of laughter" rang out. While further angering the gentleman from Kentucky, it put Hunter very much in the favor of the Republicans and, as one historian put it, "may have moved the Lincoln administration closer to openly advocating the use of black troops."[114] Throughout the summer of 1862, Hunter continued to ask for official recognition and permission to continue to raise black regiments. While his men were clothed, armed and fed, they were not officially recognized and thus did not draw any pay. Secretary of War Stanton, probably due to political pressure and also because he was getting tired of the constant requests for not only recognition of the regiment but also additional troops, refused to give Hunter a definitive answer and evaded his requests. In a letter to Stanton on August 10, Hunter, who had finally had enough, informed him that he had disbanded the First South Carolina, save for one company that had been detailed to St. Simon Island and hadn't received word of the disbanding.[115]

Hunter, disillusioned with his situation, decided to ask for another assignment. Unbeknown to him, the political climate was quickly changing in Washington in regards to arming blacks for active duty. After the Confiscation Act and the Militia Act were passed in mid-July, Stanton asked for and received a legal opinion that Lincoln could use blacks in any way militarily that he wanted. Hunter had a meeting with Saxton and Rear Admiral Samuel Du Pont on August 9. A letter again making an appeal for a black regiment and signed by General Saxton was to be hand-delivered to Stanton.[116]

Hunter turned the reins of the Department of the South over to Brigadier General John M. Brannan on August 22, 1862. Hunter requested reassignment and was given sixty days leave, during which he presided over the court-martial of General Fitzjohn Porter. On August 25, Secretary of War Stanton replied to Saxton's August 16 letter, authorizing Saxton to raise a regiment not to exceed five thousand men and to furnish them with the arms, uniforms and equipment they would need. Saxton got around the direct application for a regiment by asking to employ in the quartermaster's department a force not exceeding five thousand. Stanton's reasoning for the arming of the blacks was for the protection of the plantations and settlements. Stanton further gave Saxton orders that would allow him to use "every means within your power to withdraw from the enemy their laboring force and population, and to spare no effort consistent with civilized warfare to weaken, harass, and annoy them." Now, Saxton had the permission Hunter had longed for—permission to raise black regiments and take them to the enemy.[117]

On January 21, 1863, Major General David Hunter was ordered back to the Department of the South. He had his regiments—now it was time to recruit the men necessary to fill them and, more importantly, to deploy them.[118]

CHAPTER 5

NEW REGIMENTS

Now that Saxton had orders to raise five regiments, he set out to fill the ranks. Saxton had better relations with the superintendents of the plantations than did the somewhat autocratic and aloof Hunter. Saxton also did not believe that forcing the men to enlist would be fair or in the best interest of the regiment. Hunter felt that all freedmen should we willing to fight for their freedom, if not voluntarily then via a draft. Consequently, Saxton took on the task of visiting each plantation to recruit his men. Unbeknownst to Saxton, Captain Charles Trowbridge at this time still held a company of the original regiment on St. Simons Island. Upon learning that this company was still in existence, Saxton made it the nucleus of the First South Carolina, Company A.[119]

Saxton's attempt to raise the new regiment was hampered by the failure of the first regiment. Keeping in mind that the soldiers had never been paid, Saxton used Stanton's orders as a basis to assure the recruits that the U.S. government would indeed pay them. Many of the men in the initial regiment, as well as in this new regiment, had families, and joining the regiment meant that their families had to make their own way until the men were paid.[120]

While recruitment was slower than anticipated, the regiment did begin to take shape, enough so that Saxton began looking for a permanent commander for the regiment. During his search, he was recommended Thomas Wentworth Higginson, a radical abolitionist from Massachusetts. A student at Harvard College at the age of thirteen, Higginson was well known as a writer, minister and lecturer. He vehemently opposed the Fugitive Slave Act and participated in a number of radical acts, including trying to free an enslaved man in Boston who was to be returned south. Higginson was the only one of John Brown's Secret Six who did not flee when Brown was captured at Harpers Ferry. During the Bleeding Kansas conflict, Higginson smuggled arms to the Free-Soilers in Kansas and also met with Brown. Higginson was probably the most militant abolitionist in New England prior to the war. He advocated for a separation of the slave states from the North and opposed the war with Mexico because he believed it was just a smokescreen for the expansion of slavery. Interestingly, although Higginson had been an enthusiastic supporter of John Brown's aborted raid at Harpers

Brigadier General Rufus Saxton. *Library of Congress.*

Ferry and acknowledged the need for an armed slave insurrection, he was stiff and formal in terms of his military mindset and that of his officers—quite a contrast from his counterpart, Colonel James Montgomery.[121]

During the late 1850s, Higginson met and got to know Harriet Tubman. Writing to his mother about Tubman on December 10, 1862, from Camp Saxton, he remarked, "Who should drive out and see me today but Harriet Tubman, who is living in Beaufort as a sort of nurse and general caretaker; she sent her regards to you."[122] Camp Saxton, named for General Rufus Saxton, was located on the former Smith Plantation, about four miles from Beaufort, along the Beaufort River.

At the start of the war, Higginson volunteered to help form the Fifty-first Massachusetts Regiment, a state-sponsored regiment. While serving as captain of that regiment, he was offered the position of colonel of the First South Carolina Volunteers in Beaufort. Saxton sent him a pass so that he could visit the area and make a decision about appointment. Securing leave from Governor Andrew of Massachusetts, Higginson left the regiment he had helped create and sailed south. Within a day after arriving, Higginson accepted the commission.[123]

Higginson took over the reins of the First South Carolina and, while Saxton continued to recruit, started turning the raw recruits into proper soldiers. Higginson was a "by the book" commander, having little military experience previously. This bode especially well for the First South Carolina, as the eyes of the military and the entire nation were on them. The decorum of the unit and how it appeared to others was always on Higginson's mind. There was very much still the question of whether a regiment of former slaves could or would become a proper fighting force and actually contribute to the war effort.[124]

With the formation of the first regiment almost completed, Saxton and Hunter turned their sights on forming the second regiment.

January 1863 brought Colonel James Montgomery to the Department of the South. With the breakup of Lane's Brigade and the absorption of the Third Kansas into the Tenth Kansas, Montgomery was left on the outside. He traveled to Washington, where he was offered the position of commander of the Second South Carolina Volunteers effective January 13, 1863. He would serve alongside Higginson and under his old commander, Major General David Hunter.

Colonel James Montgomery was authorized by Secretary of War Edwin Stanton to raise a regiment, subject to Hunter's approval, to serve for three years or during the war. Arriving in Port Royal in late January, he found no regiment waiting for him. Montgomery tried, with little success, to recruit in the Sea Islands, Saxton having already thoroughly covered the area. General Hunter then gave Montgomery a pass to go to Key West, Florida, and "seize every able-bodied male contraband." Key West, held by the Union throughout the war, was a safe haven for freed slaves brought in by ships from various points.[125]

Montgomery's recruitment didn't depend on impressing the contrabands there; rather, he had enough willing recruits from the refugee camps in Key West, 125 men, to return to Port Royal. Some of these men had escaped from places as far away as St. Augustine, in the northern reaches of the state. The number of men from north Florida who volunteered in Key West probably reinforced the notion that there were large numbers of slaves just waiting to be liberated.[126]

On February 23, the Second South Carolina arrived to a prepared camp next to the camp of the First South Carolina at Camp Saxton. Local recruitment continued, Hunter apparently not having learned from his first unsuccessful attempt at impressing the men. Just prior to a movement conducted by the First and Second South Carolina Volunteers, one of the teachers on the plantation wrote, "Came home at night with the news the First South Carolina Volunteers started on an expedition today which Colonel Higginson considers of very great importance, which will have very great results, or from which they will never return. Also that drafting has begun in Beaufort by Hunter's orders."[127]

One of the plantation teachers wrote, "General Saxton has passed his word to the people here that they shall not be forced into the army."[128]

Higginson, while welcoming Montgomery, had some reservations: "I am delighted to have Montgomery for though very likely his system of drill & discipline may be more lax & western than mine; still in actual service his experience will be invaluable. This is all I can say now." Higginson would have much more to say about Montgomery after the events of June.[129]

Governor Andrew of Massachusetts, writing a few months later in a recommendation for a commander of his Massachusetts troops to Secretary Stanton, summed up the feelings of many concerning Higginson and Montgomery: "Higginson, the senior colonel of the brigade, although a brave and chivalrous gentleman of high culture, has never seen much service, and never any in the field until he went to South Carolina. Montgomery, the next in rank, undoubtedly a valuable man and very useful as a good bushwhacker, is hardly a competent brigadier."[130]

While Governor Andrew had some political reasons for his letter to Stanton, he could not have been so naive when he referred to Montgomery as a "bushwhacker," a term that was almost exclusively reserved for the proslavery ruffians from Missouri.

Trial by Fire

By the time the Second South Carolina was being formed, the First South Carolina Volunteers had gone on expeditions to Doughboy Island and a foray up the St. Mary's River on January 21. In the raid up the St. Mary's, the regiment came under fire for the first time. Higginson was elated at the response of his troops: "Nobody knows anything about these men who has not seen them under fire." Expecting to find large numbers of contrabands, Higginson instead found few slaves anywhere, the countryside being deserted.[131]

While in camp at Beaufort on March 5, Higginson was ordered to take his First South Carolina Volunteers, about 860 men, and Montgomery and his 120 men, supported by the Seventh Connecticut Regiment, to occupy Jacksonville. The intended purpose of the mission was to "carry the proclamation of freedom to the enslaved; to call all loyal men into the service of the United States; to occupy as much of the State of Florida as possible with the forces under your command; and to neglect no means consistent with the usages of civilized warfare to weaken, harass, and annoy those who are in rebellion against the Government of the United States." Of course, "loyal men" meant slaves and free blacks.[132]

Hunter had more than just an expedition to Jacksonville on his mind. He issued orders for his troops to be ready for a major movement against the Confederates. He also formally re-instituted the draft of contrabands. Saxton was strongly opposed to Hunter's draft. He knew it would not work; the men drafted would not have the enthusiasm nor the determination to do their jobs. As a consequence, many took to the woods to avoid being drafted, and many of those who were drafted later deserted.[133]

When Montgomery left Beaufort with Higginson and his First South Carolina Volunteers, he had fewer than 120 ill-trained troops with him. They had not been issued arms, and it wasn't until they reached Fernandina that Montgomery's men finally had a way to defend themselves.[134]

Montgomery's men (only 66 of whom were effective) encamped in a deserted house on the western outskirts of Jacksonville. The following morning, the men were put to work learning to drill and to shoulder arms. While the men were training, Montgomery heard firing from his pickets. In an open area about a mile from camp, the Confederates had staged their men for an attack. As the pickets fell back, the Confederate cavalry came in a charge, opening fire from about three hundred yards away. The men of the Second South Carolina took the brunt of the fight, aided by men from the First Regiment. The men held their ground and returned fire, stopping the advance of the Confederates. Running short on ammunition, the Second Regiment pulled back closer to town. At a nearby wooded area, they regrouped and then slowly advanced, knowing they were up against superior numbers, to find the Confederate cavalry gone. In their place was a line of Confederate infantry advancing across the field. The Federals returned fire once again and were again ordered to fall back to the protection of the gunboats. After a few rounds of artillery from the gunboats, the Confederates vacated the field.[135]

In his diary, Captain William Lee Apthorp of the Second South Carolina wrote, "They did not succeed in capturing the Jayhawker and his niggers as they had hoped, but on the contrary began to think that a black man could stand up and pull a trigger and that a bullet from his rifle was as deadly a thing to receive as if a white man had fired it." Once again, it was proved that the new soldiers would fight and fight effectively.[136]

Once Jacksonville was secured, the First South Carolina garrisoned the town. The Second South Carolina had a different mission. Montgomery was to take his men up the river to fulfill the orders Saxton had given earlier—mainly to recruit and free any slaves found and to harass and economically damage the enemy. Higginson also wanted Montgomery to open the small port town of Palatka for possible use as a base of operations.

The men of the Second Regiment departed on the armed transport *General Burnside* and slowly made their way upriver. The troops managed to capture a Confederate colonel, as well as a large amount of livestock and poultry. They returned to Jacksonville with their prizes. Meeting the boat, Higginson described the scene onboard the ship: "The steamer seemed an animated hen-coop. Live poultry hung from the foremast shrouds, dead ones from the mainmast, geese hissed from the binnacle, a pig paced the quarter-deck, and a duck's wings were seen fluttering from a line which was wont to sustain duck trousers." While disapproving of Montgomery's habits on these raids, he nevertheless ingratiated himself to the naval officers when he and his men presented them with some choice turkeys and ducks.[137]

A few days later, the Second Regiment left again on a raid up the river, this time traveling aboard the *General Meigs*. They stopped at Mandarin, Orange Mills, Palatka and Doctors Lake. Here, about six miles from the river, Montgomery and thirty-four men were able to capture a Confederate lieutenant and fifteen of his men, a group of partisan rangers and nine and a half bales of cotton. Montgomery's men were able to liberate some thirty slaves as well. Upon arriving back at the transport the following morning with their prisoners—less the lieutenant, who had escaped on the way back—they men learned they were to be recalled and returned to Jacksonville. On the trip back to Jacksonville, they confiscated another three and a half bales of cotton from a scow.[138]

March 29 brought the Union evacuation of Jacksonville, with the last of the men leaving on the thirty-first. General Hunter, who had been planning an attack on Charleston, had been imploring the War Department for additional troops for months. Receiving no response, however, he found himself having to recall his units from Florida. The units under Higginson and Montgomery had displayed courage under fire and had proven themselves equal to any other regiment in the Union.[139]

CHAPTER 6

THE LOWCOUNTRY

This expedition is but the initial experiment of a system of incursions which will
penetrate up all the inlets, creeks, and rivers of this department.
—*General David Hunter, Department of the South, June 3, 1863*

The South Carolina coast consists of barrier islands fronted by sandy beaches and sand dunes leading to shallow coastal waters. Most of these islands have scattered, heavily wooded areas and the occasional freshwater swamp. The rear of these islands evolves into wide expanses of impenetrable salt marsh broken up by small tidal creeks. Farther inland, the rivers emerge to break up the higher land into innumerable islands and peninsulas. The rivers along the coastal plain are tidal, for the most part, with many navigable for upward of twenty miles.

Separating these barrier islands are numerous natural harbors and sounds. Principal entrances include Bulls Bay, Charleston Harbor, St. Helena Sound and Port Royal Sound. Rivers emptying into the harbors and sounds include the Sampit River in Georgetown County; the Ashley, Stono and Cooper Rivers in Charleston County; the Broad River in Beaufort County; and the Ashepoo, Combahee and North and South Edisto Rivers in Colleton County.

The southern South Carolina coast was protected by numerous hastily built earthen forts, namely Fort Walker on Hilton Head and Fort Beauregard on Bay Point, both of which guarded the entrance to Port Royal Sound, and another on Otter Island defending the entrance to St. Helena Sound.

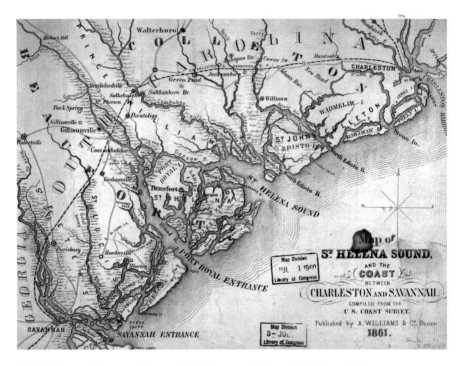

An 1861 map of the coast between Charleston and Savannah. *Library of Congress.*

A smaller unnamed work was erected at the mouth of the Ashepoo River, on Fenwick Island adjacent to the fort on Otter Island, and others on Edisto Island guarded the North and South Edisto Inlets.

On November 7, 1861, a Federal force, led by Flag Officer S.F. DuPont, and the Union fleet attacked the Confederate defenders at Port Royal. Running midway between Forts Walker and Beauregard, giving and receiving fire from both forts and then turning two and a half miles north and running back closer to Fort Walker, the fleet could bring all its guns to bear on the weakest side of Fort Walker. At the same time, other ships stood off, raking the sea faces of the fort.[140]

The Confederates fought gallantly, but the much heavier guns of the Federal fleet soon overcame Fort Walker. After only four hours, its guns fell silent, and by 2:20 p.m., the Union flag flew over the fort. Fort Beauregard soon ceased firing as well. By noon the following day, Fort Beauregard had been turned over to Union general Isaac I. Stevens.[141]

The fall of Port Royal delivered to the Federal forces one of the finest harbors in the South, giving them not only the success of the blockade but also a much-needed base of operations for attacks against Charleston, Savannah and Florida. The harbor and surrounding lands also gave them a base for coaling stations, repair shops and supply depots. Eventually, it would provide a refuge for thousands of escaping slaves from the surrounding plantations.

Immediately, the Confederate forces abandoned all the coastal earthen forts, withdrawing to the mainland interior, protected by rivers and swamps.

Confusion reigned in the southern counties as General Robert E. Lee headed south from Charleston on the Charleston and Savannah Railroad. Lee, recently transferred from Western Virginia to Richmond and now to the Department of South Carolina, Georgia and East Florida, faced a difficult task: defending the coast from the Federals.[142]

Lee arrived to a scene of confusion in Coosawhatchie, as General R.S. Ripley, the local commander, was headed to the front. After surveying the retreat from Port Royal, Ripley rode to Coosawhatchie to confer with Lee, reporting the fall of Port Royal. While the Confederates were able to withdraw their troops to the mainland, they lost all of their supplies, ammunition and the cannon in both Fort Beauregard and Fort Walker.[143]

Lee assessed his situation and took stock of his assets. He had about seven thousand troops, most of whom were untrained and ill-equipped; very few cannon; and no way (other than the geography of the area) to stop the Federal advance. The Federals now controlled all of the Sea Islands and all inland waterways separating the Sea Islands from the mainland. To make matters worse, the Charleston and Savannah Railroad connecting the two cities was located just inland from navigable waters. If the Federals were able to mount an attack and cut the railroad, they could easily attack either city from the rear without the Confederates being able to reinforce the troops from either city. Lee determined the railroad must be protected at all costs.

In a letter to the adjutant general in Richmond a few months later, Lee summed up his situation:

> *Wherever his* [the enemy's] *fleet can be brought, no opposition to his landing can be made except within range of our fixed batteries. We have nothing to oppose its heavy guns, which sweep over the low banks of the country with irresistible force. The further he can be withdrawn from his floating batteries, the weaker he will become.*[144]

To protect his troops and the railroad, Lee withdrew his men to the Charleston and Savannah Railroad. Lee was probably influenced greatly by a report written in 1826 by Major Joseph G. Totten that detailed a national coastal defense. Totten wrote of harbor forts that delayed the attacking enemy until local troops could be brought to bear. To this theory, Lee added the element of rail transportation. In this manner, large garrisons could be kept at Charleston and Savannah to deter initial attacks with additional troops coming from either city as reinforcements. To protect the railroad itself, additional troops would be held in camp at strategic locations along the railroad to defend against local incursions of the enemy, again with reinforcements coming from Charleston or Savannah or both.

Lee also removed the last Confederate troops and artillery from forward earthworks on Edisto Island, Sam's Point, Otter Island and Fenwick Island, leaving behind the destroyed works Colonel Ambrosio Gonzales, Confederate chief of artillery, had recently reinforced.[145]

To strengthen the defenses of the Charleston and Savannah Railroad, Lee established armed camps along the railroad at Coosawhatchie, Pocotaligo, Adams Run and Green Pond, with minor camps at the Ashepoo. Lee also set out to reinforce and protect the rivers with a series of batteries and obstructions placed in the rivers.[146]

The philosophy related by Totten and adapted by Lee, along with the "Flying Siege Train," a mobile artillery unit, as expressed by Colonel Gonzales, suited the physical properties of the land and rivers but also took into consideration the climate of coastal South Carolina. Often overlooked in discussions of the coastal fortifications of South Carolina is the prevalence of disease.[147]

The climate of South Carolina consists of mild winters and hot, humid summers. The area south and east of the Charleston and Savannah Railroad was dominated by vast areas of inland swamps and rice fields, reclaimed from hardwood swamps and marshes. The period from late May until the first frost was referred to as the "sickly season" due to the high rates of infectious diseases such as yellow fever and malaria. While early in the war construction didn't stop during the "sickly season," the actual manning of these batteries ceased due to the prevalence of disease, and the troops withdrew to camps along the railroad. It was during the "sickly season" that the planters moved their families from the coast to more healthy inland cities and towns. In this time, mosquitoes were not known as vectors of disease, the prevailing notion being that the "vapors" from the lowlands caused diseases.

As the Confederate troops were pulled back from these batteries and camps, they left pickets in their place to warn of any Federal incursions. Regular cavalry patrols were made of the various picket posts and batteries.

If the enemy were spotted, the alarm would go out to the encampments at Pocotaligo, Green Pond, Ballouville or Coosawhatchie via mounted pickets and telegraph. The Confederates would respond with cavalry, infantry and field artillery. If there was a large incursion by the Union forces, troops and armaments from other depots along the railroad would respond. In addition, some of the batteries did have standing installations of cannon and supplies; however, this varied throughout the war, as the armaments were needed at various other points, with much being sent north to Virginia.[148]

Early in the war, abundant slave labor, as well as infantry, was used to construct these fortifications. This allowed the luxury of large structures with deep, wide ditches and interior structures such as bombproofs.

In a letter home from Camp Heywood on March 8, 1863, Private Samuel McKetterick, Company B, Allston's Company, First Battalion, South Carolina Sharpshooters, writes of the work on the large battery under construction at Combahee Ferry: "We have to guard the Negros that are working on the breastworks…There was a call for 30 men from our ay [*sic*] to work on the Battery today."[149]

Later, due to lack of manpower and smaller cannon on the Federal gunboats, as well as a lack of cannon of significant caliber, the Confederates abandoned the massive earthworks used early in the war in favor of works designed for field artillery and infantry.[150]

Initially, the fortifications just upriver of the sounds were enlarged to provide for the lessons learned by the fall of Forts Beauregard and Walker. The fortification on the Ashepoo River, Fort Chapman, was one of these. In large contrast to later river fortifications, it was constructed on a bend in the Ashepoo River on Chapman's Plantation and consisted of two widely separated gun emplacements joined by a large earthen curtain. Immediately to the rear of each of these emplacements were large magazines, or bombproofs.[151]

Continuing throughout the war, many small batteries were built along the rivers, swamps and roads to protect from Federal raids, as well as in response to attempts to cut the Charleston and Savannah Railroad. In Colleton County and northern Beaufort County

a small battery and blockhouse was built at Fields Point, also known as Combahee Point, at the entrance to the Combahee River. A small work was placed at Tar Bluff a few miles above the earthworks at Fields Point on a bend in the river, and a large fort was located at Combahee Ferry to protect the highway connecting Port Royal Ferry to the Savannah–Charleston road.

Fortifications were also built across roads to prevent land movement, such as the battery on the road from Fields Point to the Charleston Road.[152]

In order to fully understand the Combahee River Raid and the part the differing parties played, one first has to understand the lay of the land as it was in 1863.

The Combahee River is a narrow, meandering tidal river that empties into St. Helena Sound. From the mouth of the river to Combahee Ferry, the present-day U.S. Highway 17, it is approximately twenty-five miles by river and about ten to twelve miles by land.

To the south and west of the river lies Beaufort County. The river is separated from the high land mostly by wide expanses (sometimes over two miles wide) of marsh.

On the northeast side of the river is Colleton County. Here, the river follows a course that brings it in proximity to the upland areas. Nearer to the mouth of the river, the land is composed of high bluffs separated by deep ravines. This is the area where Middleton Bluff and Tar Bluff are located. The tip of this land is called Fields Point.

Upstream from the bluff areas, the river starts to lose its salinity and height (although it is still tidal), and the freshwater swamps start to appear. This is the area known as the "fertile valley of the Combahee." These swamps were historically composed of hardwood trees, mostly tupelo, gum and cypress. Beginning in the late 1600s, these swamps were gradually cleared for the cultivation of rice.[153]

The land adjacent to the Combahee River on the Colleton side is actually a peninsula. On the southwest is the Combahee River and on the northeast the Chehaw River. The only through road down this peninsula is what today is known as Stocks Creek Road. This road starts near Fields Point, runs north toward Tar Bluff, turns northeast toward the Chehaw River and then, after crossing a small causeway, parallels the Chehaw. While it starts at the Combahee River, it ends up on the Combahee–Ashepoo Road, presently known as U.S. 17, approximately five miles from the Combahee River. Other than individual roads and tracks used by the different plantations, there were no other through roads in 1863.

The rice plantations along the Combahee were located upstream within a few miles of the Combahee Ferry. Lower portions of the river were too saline for rice production, although cotton and vegetables were grown. The most productive lands were near the ferry itself. Here, the rice fields were one mile wide. The ferry itself was established formally in 1714. The causeway was

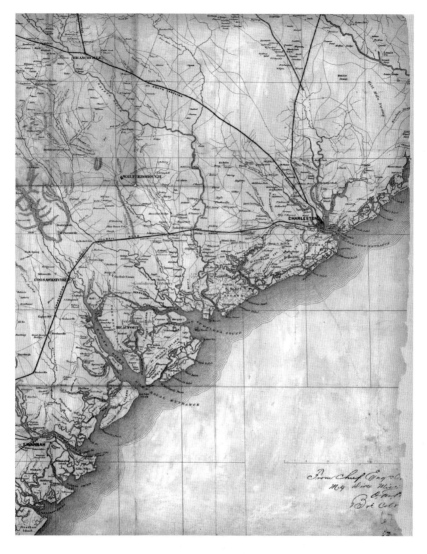

A map showing the principal locations at the time of the raid (tracing of a map in *Robert Mills' Atlas*). *Library of Congress.*

defined upon its establishment, with a width of sixteen feet. The river is on the west side of these rice fields.[154]

The rice fields were large, diked areas broken only by canals to allow for the shipment of rice to the mills and for access to the main compound. Harvest time for both rice and cotton was in the fall. June would have been the middle of the growing season.

The river was the main "highway" for these plantations.

Most of the Chehaw Neck, as the area was known, was cleared for agricultural uses, the clearings broken only by stands of live oaks and some pinelands, particularly in the interior. Despite what is commonly thought, where were no "grand" houses—like the one portrayed in the motion picture *Gone with the Wind*—on the neck, as the planters had their large homes in Beaufort, Charleston, Walterboro and Savannah. There were few houses we would consider "upscale" today, and all were of wood construction.

During the war, the Confederates, beginning in 1861 and 1862, established a network of campsites, batteries, rifle trenches and blockhouses. Every major landing point along the Combahee River was fortified. At Fields Point, there was a blockhouse, rifle trenches and a small battery. This position overlooked the mouth of the Combahee and gave a vista of over ten miles. At Tar Bluff, there was also a small battery.[155]

At the causeway at Stocks Creek, there was a network of two batteries connected by rifle trenches. To the west across the creek was another battery protecting the approaches from Middleton Bluff.[156] There were also two extensive sets of lines known as the Lower Chehaw Lines and the Ashepoo Lines, which extended from the Combahee to the Ashepoo River to the East.[157] Nearby at Lowndes Mill was a large three-gun battery, which was

The site of the Combahee Ferry and rice fields, 2014. *Photograph by Jeff W. Grigg.*

connected via rifle trenches running north to another battery that straddled the Combahee–Ashepoo Road.[158]

On the Beaufort side of the river, the only place where the river approached land was in the vicinity of Combahee Ferry. Here was located another large battery with rifle trenches as well as small batteries at the ferry and the north side of the small island that composed Combahee Ferry.[159]

Major camps for the Confederates were in Pocotaligo, Green Pond, Ashepoo and Adams Run. The Charleston and Savannah Railroad ran a few miles to the west and north of this area, making an arc from Charleston to Savannah. No Confederate camps, storehouses, munitions or any other military assets were affected by the raid.

Chapter 7

A DIFFERENT KIND OF WARFARE

The New York Tribune *says that the negro troops at Hilton Head, S.C., will soon start an expedition, under the command of Colonel Montgomery, different in many respects from any heretofore projected.*[160]

The Department of the South was in many respects different from any other theater of the war. Although the Union controlled the Sea Islands immediately around Port Royal and St. Helena Sound to the north and St. Simon Island to the south, it did not control the area on the mainland, and it wouldn't until General W.T. Sherman's march from Savannah to Columbia in 1865. From the beginning, Port Royal was to be the Southern depot for the South Atlantic Blockading Squadron. Here, the ships could be resupplied and repaired and also provide hospital facilities. It was also an army base from which to stage attacks on the nearby cities of Charleston, Savannah and Jacksonville. Also, Port Royal by default became the largest safe area for escaping slaves, known as contrabands.

While organizing the First South Carolina Volunteers, General Saxton devised, most likely in concert with General Hunter, a new type of warfare. It was a philosophy born from the surrounding countryside and the desire to both take the fight to the Confederates and free large numbers of enslaved people. This worked for Saxton in two ways: (1) as an abolitionist and (2) to fill the ranks of his five regiments. This type of raid was an outgrowth of the Florida expeditions and characteristic of Hunter's and particularly Montgomery's mindset as to warfare in the Department of the South.

Here along the southeast coast, it wasn't merely a matter of assembling your troops and marching forward; it was island hopping and transporting your army via small boats, flats and ships. Lines of supply were difficult, and there were very real hazards, such as torpedoes, to contend with in the rivers. Each expedition could only go so far up the rivers, and when the soldiers disembarked on land, they had to stay close to the river or have no artillery protection. Without the protection of the large guns on the gunboats, the Federals would be left exposed and vulnerable.

Hunter also understood that without being able to establish a base of supply on the mainland and keep a large enough garrison, he couldn't hold the ground. Any competent commander fully understood that he could not hold a piece of ground with only the rivers and marsh at his back. The Confederates would be able to bring large numbers of men, artillery and supplies and quickly capture and defeat any force that languished in the area for long.

In response to this reality, the Union generals devised a different type of warfare in the Department of the South. They would establish a base of operations and then go forth to raid the countryside. Hopefully, this would cause the Confederates to abandon the area. In this manner, few troops could control a large area. It worked in Florida, but not in South Carolina. The Confederates were just too strong and the logistics too difficult.

In a letter to Secretary of War Stanton, Saxton outlined briefly his thoughts: "These boats should go up the streams, land at the different plantations, drive in the pickets, and capture them if possible. The blowing of the steamer's whistle the negroes all understand as a signal to come in." The Union commander felt not only that they could fill the regiments but that they sought to punish the planters as well.[161]

While logistics stymied the Union, a number of issues kept the Confederates from successfully defending the mainland between Savannah and Charleston, including a lack of manpower, a lack of guns (cannon), inexperienced troops and the "sickly season." Few of the earthworks had cannon, and many were defended only by a few pickets. Some outlying earthworks were not manned by soldiers but instead depended on cavalry to patrol them, the idea being that the pickets or cavalry would have ample time to raise the alarm at the large camps, after which the troops could respond en masse. The area as a whole was under close observation with the Confederate cavalry's constant patrolling of the roads and men stationed at critical posts. In the previous months, the Fifth South Carolina Cavalry, which had been stationed in the area and knew it well, had been rotated out and the Fourth South Carolina Cavalry, lately stationed in the First Military District, Georgetown, and the Rutledge Mounted Rifles and Horse Artillery moved in. South Carolina was divided into four military districts. The areas of Green Pond and Combahee Ferry were in the Third Military District, commanded by Brigadier General W.S. Walker.[162]

Some of the installations temporarily abandoned by the Confederates would have prevented much of the raid, these being Ballouville, three and a half miles east of the ferry on the Charleston road, and a camp three miles up the road from Fields Point. Both of these stations were abandoned during the summer due to the "extreme unhealthiness" of the area. The troops stationed there were sent to camp at Green Pond on the Charleston and Savannah Railroad, about eight miles from the ferry.[163]

In early May, the heavy cannon were removed from the earthworks along the rivers in the district, the unhealthy climate and lack of proper supporting troops for the artillery being the chief reasons for their removal. Just two weeks before the raid, General P.G.T. Beauregard ordered the guns transferred to Savannah, where they were to be held until needed again. To replace the large cannon, General Walker recommended that rifled field guns be supplied, adding that these could be handled by either artillerists in the field or infantry soldiers. He specifically recommended guns for the Combahee and Ashepoo Rivers. Colonel Ambrosio Gonzales, Confederate chief of artillery and ordnance, replied that there were no guns available but that Shultz's Battery in the Second Military District could possibly be moved. He also informed Walker that as soon as some Napoleon guns could be procured, they could be put in position on the Chehaw Neck. (The Chehaw Neck is the area bounded on the west by the Combahee River and on the east by the Ashepoo River. It is an area of mainly high ground, but in the lower reaches, it is split by the Chehaw River and associated swamps.[164]) In the meantime, this left the rivers of the district lightly defended from a Union attack.

Hdqrs. Third District So. Car.
McPhersonville, May 18, 1863
Brig. Gen. Thomas Jordan
Chief of Staff and Assistant Adjutant-General

General:
In view of the withdrawal of the heavy batteries from the rivers in this district, both on account of their want of support and the extreme

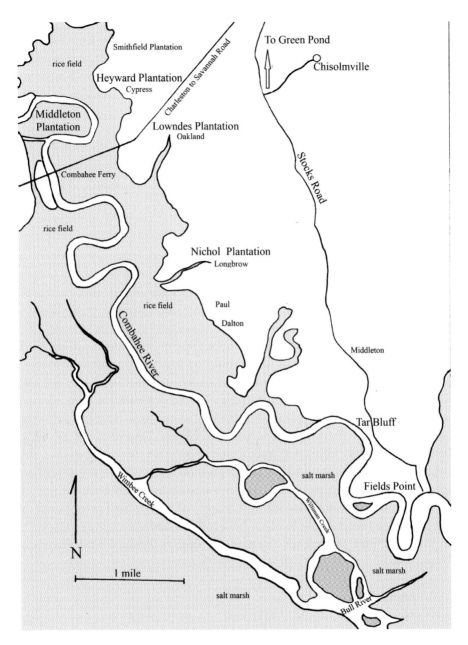

Map of the Combahee River showing plantations affected by the raid. *Map by Jeff W. Grigg.*

unhealthiness of the localities in which they are placed, I would respectfully recommend that field rifled guns be supplied for that purpose. They could be manned by companies of light artillery or by instructed infantry encamped in the vicinity. I would recommend the guns to be sent for the defense of the followings points: Combahee and Ashepoo Rivers (the same guns would serve both points), Coosawhatchie and Red Bluff.

I have the honor to be, very respectfully, your obedient servant,

W.S. Walker
Brigadier-General, Commanding[165]

Hdqrs. Chief of Arty. and Ord.
Charleston, May 21, 1863

Respectfully returned.
    There are no batteries available for the purposes here within mentioned but those of Captain Gaillard in the First Military District and Captain Schulz in the Second District; neither are there any rifle guns in the depot unassigned or provided with ammunition.
    The defense of the Combahee and Ashepoo is so important that I would suggest the removal of Shulz's [sic] battery to Combahee Neck and the transfer of Culpeper's battery to the Second Military District.
    As soon as Napoleon guns are procured, of which four will soon be cast at the Charleston Arsenal, I will have the honor earnestly to advocate, for the purpose of meeting the very want of our seaboard in the summer months, referred to by General Walker, the formation of batteries of horse artillery, with four Napoleon guns each and eight horses to the piece, and the Beaufort Artillery would answer admirably for such a purpose in the Third Military District. Such a battery would be far preferable to one of rifle guns for every purpose of attack or defense above the mouths of our principal rivers.

A.J. Gonzales
Colonel and Chief of Arty. and Ord.[166]

The Confederates had ample warning that something was afoot in the Third District. The previous year, it had been reported that a group of twenty-five Union troops exchanged fire with two or three Confederate pickets at one of William Heyward's plantations on the lower Combahee River. Northern newspapers also gave warning. A month earlier, the *New York Tribune* had stated, "The negro troops at Hilton Head, S.C., will soon start upon an expedition, under the commend of Colonel Montgomery, different in many respects from any heretofore projected." The Confederates had copies of these newspapers and distributed warnings to the commands in the field.[167]

On May 26, the Confederate pickets received special orders from McPhersonville warning that if there were any more false alarms, they would be court-martialed. The orders further stated that if the enemy did show and they failed to keep in close contact, they would be subject to "the charge of cowardice and to be tried by court-martial." This order was in response to a number of false alarms in the Third District. So, while they should have been more alert, at the same time, they were less likely to raise an alarm until absolutely certain of the situation. McPhersonville was the largest camp in the Third District and was about twenty miles south of Green Pond on the Charleston and Savannah Railroad.[168]

On May 27, a circular was issued to the planters in the Third District and posted at railroad stations. It read: "It is the wish of the commanding general that you advise all planters and owners of negroes in your military district to remove their negroes as far as practicable into the interior of the State, as otherwise they are liable to be lost at any moment." Yet few planters in the district paid much attention; it was, after all, the height of the rice-growing season, and all hands were needed in the fields. If they removed their slaves, there would be no crop that year, which would be economically disastrous.[169]

The three army transports—the *John Adams*, a converted ferryboat of the East Boston Line; the *Harriet A. Weed*, a steam tug and troop transport; and the *Sentinel*—lay quietly at the wharf in Beaufort. Both the *John Adams* and the *Harriet A. Weed* were armed. The *John Adams* was the most heavily armed, with both a ten- and a twenty-pounder Parrott gun and two howitzers, while the *Harriet A. Weed* carried two cannon.[170]

The guns on these boats were manned by the Third Rhode Island Heavy Artillery, Company C, under Captain Charles R. Brayton. The Third Rhode Island manned the guns on most of the inland gunboats assigned to the army, of which virtually all were converted from civilian use. The *John Adams*, being a converted double side-wheel steamer, was uniquely suited for patrolling and transporting on the shallow rivers and bays of the Department of the South. Its large carrying capacity,

THE COMBAHEE RIVER RAID

RAID OF SECOND SOUTH CAROLINA VOLUNTEERS (COL. MONTGOMERY) AMONG THE RICE PLANTATIONS ON THE COMBAHEE, S. C.—[SEE PAGE 427.]

Montgomery's Raid on the Combahee. *From* Harper's Weekly, *July 4, 1863.*

maneuverability and stable platform allowed it to carry the troops and guns easily.

Leaving at dark on June 1, the small flotilla sailed up the Beaufort River toward the Coosaw River and then on to the St. Helena Sound and up the Combahee River. Once leaving the confines of the Beaufort River, the Coosaw was an open tidal river flowing into St. Helena Sound. Here, near the mouth of the Coosaw, was the Combahee River, also emptying into the sound. Shortly after leaving the dock, the *Sentinel* ran aground (this was to become an all-too-common problem for the *Sentinel*). The men and material from the *Sentinel* were transferred to the two other ships, leaving the stranded ship behind and delaying the expedition. The *John Adams* and the *Harriet A. Weed* steamed across the open water with no moon to mark their silhouettes (being a last-quarter moon, it would not rise until midnight, and it wouldn't reach its highest point until dawn).[171]

Montgomery's force consisted of the men of the Third Rhode Island Heavy Artillery and about 250 of the Second South Carolina Volunteers, under Captains Thomas N. Thompson, James M. Carver, William Apthorp and John M. Adams. Since the Jacksonville expedition in the Port Royal area, a total of 150 men had been recruited into the Second South Carolina. A total force of approximately 300 regular men and officers departed on the two ships.[172]

Accompanying Montgomery was Harriet Tubman and two of her pilots, Charles Simmons and Samuel Hayward, both of whom were familiar with the area. Both Tubman and Montgomery would have been in the pilothouse of the *John Adams*, the lead vessel, mindful of the fate of its previous captain, Captain Clifton, who had been killed by a sharpshooter in Florida a few months earlier. Most likely, Samuel Hayward had recently escaped from one of William Heyward's plantations on the Combahee. The latter wrote in his diary, "In March, fifteen of my negroes, including three women and one child, left the plantation and went over to the enemy on the islands."[173]

On reaching the mouth of the Coosaw, the salt marshes spread out in front of them. Unlike northern rivers, the banks of the rivers in this area near the sea were flanked by wide expanses of marsh grass only a few feet above the water, providing no cover. The two ships slowly made their way into the Combahee and traveled another two miles upstream until coming to the first high land, Fields Point. The ships advanced to the edge of the river and unloaded a small force under Captain Thompson at dawn. Montgomery left Captain Thompson and his men. Finding the Confederate earthworks abandoned, Thompson occupied the fortifications defending the landing and sought out the Confederates.[174] (An earthwork is a man-made earthen fortification used to protect artillery or, in the case of a rifle pit, a trench line for the protection of infantry. These features could be combined in various ways depending on the artillery and infantry used. A breastwork is a small earthwork that could be used by both artillery and infantry.[175])

Montgomery's plans were simple and effective. At every landing, his troops would disembark, push back any Confederates and then hold the area. Being on a peninsula, he had little to fear from a flanking movement of the Confederates. The Confederates could attack from only one direction. With each stop, the Union forces would open a new front, thereby spreading the possible counterattack thin and further reducing the effectiveness of the Confederates. Once Montgomery's objective had been reached and the destruction done, Montgomery would pull back downriver, removing his men and the fleeing slaves as he went. The men on shore would slowly pull back to the landings, preventing the Confederates from bringing up any effective artillery. The overall strategy was to make a lightning-fast strike

Fields Point and Tar Bluff looking south. *Photo by Jeff W. Grigg.*

upriver, throw the Confederates into confusion and then, before an effective counterstrike could be made, pull off out of reach of the Confederates.

At Fields Point, the Confederates had placed five pickets under Lance Corporal Newton. Newton reported that at around 3:00 a.m. on the morning of the second, he saw the gunboats slowly steaming up the river about two miles distant. The pickets at Fields Point watched the boats until they came near, at which time Newton mounted his men and fell back three hundred yards. After leaving his men, Newton cautiously returned on foot to the point, where he saw eight to twelve men land. Hearing other men being transported to shore, Newton sent a courier up the Stokes (Stocks) Road about ten miles to Lieutenant William E. Hewitt, Fourth South Carolina Cavalry, at Chisolmville.[176] (In reports, the road and causeway leading from Fields Point and Tar Bluff to Green Pond was referred to as "Stokes Road." The actual name was "Stocks Road," named for the Stocks family who had established a plantation there in colonial days. Chisolmville was a small settlement near the March Plantation midway between Fields Point and Green Pond. Used as a temporary camp by the Confederates, it is located in the present-day Donnelly Wildlife Management area.)

Captain Thompson's men, landing at Fields Point, spotted the five retreating pickets and cautiously followed them for about one and a half miles up the road, neither side firing. Proceeding farther upriver with both ships, as the Federals rounded a long, narrow bend in the river, they found before them the twenty-foot-high Tar Bluff, topped by a small unmanned battery and rifle pits. Montgomery ordered Captain Carver and his company to go ashore and guard the bluff, the only other road from the point.[177]

Leaving men at Tar Bluff and Fields Point, Montgomery and the two gunboats steamed up the Combahee. Their next stop was the plantation of Joshua Nicholls. Surprised at the sudden appearance of the gunboats, Nicholls's overseers rode off, leaving the hands in the fields. The *Weed* pulled up to the shore, and the troops under Captains Apthorp and Adams landed, quickly throwing out skirmishers to guard against a Confederate counterattack. The pickets of Apthorp's company, the lead group, advanced up the river and skirmished with the Confederates, with one casualty on the Confederate side and one contraband killed in the crossfire.[178]

The Union forces set to burning the large stores of rice, as well as the barns and plantation residences, leaving no building standing. The men of the Second South Carolina opened and destroyed the floodgates (rice trunks), flooding the fields. Rice mills were torched until only their darkened

View of the Combahee River from Tar Bluff. *Photo by Jeff W. Grigg.*

chimneys remained. As they went about their methodical destruction of the plantation, the slaves streamed down to the transport.

Harper's Weekly printed one Union soldier's account of the raid: "We skirmished all day with the rebels, but escaped without the loss of a man. Their cavalry killed and wounded some of the slaves as they swarmed to the protection of the old flag."[179] Captain Apthorp described the joy of the newly freed slaves: "They rushed toward us running over with delight, and overwhelming us with blessings. 'Lord bless you, Massa,' they would cry, often with tears running down their dark cheeks and clinging to our hands, knees, clothing, and weapons. 'De Lord bless you. We been expecting you and prayin' for you this long time! Oh Massa, tank de Lord you come at last! Good morning Massa. Oh bless the good Lord.'"[180]

In her biography after the war, Harriet Tubman described the scene of the slaves escaping to the boats:

> *I nebber see such a sight. We laughed, an' laughed, an' laughed. Here you'd see a woman wid a pail on her head, rice a smokin' in it jus' as she'd taken it from de fire, young one hangin' on behind, one han' roun' her forehead to hold on, t'other han' diggin' into de rice-pot, eatin' wid all its might; hold of her dress two or three more; down her back a bag wid a pig in it. One woman brought two pigs, a white one an' a black one; we took 'em all on board; named de white pig Beauregard, and de black pig Jeff Davis. Sometimes de women would come wid twins hangin' roun' der necks; 'pears like I nebber see so many twins in my life; bags on der shoulders, baskets on der heads, and young ones taggin' behin', all loaded; pigs squealin', chickens screamin', young ones squallin'.[181]*

Leaving Major Corwin in charge of the *Weed*, Montgomery on the *John Adams* proceeded farther upstream. The Confederates were in disarray. The pickets from Fields Point had fallen back one and a half miles from their post without putting up any resistance. The courier from Fields Point made his way to Chisolmville, where Lieutenant W.E. Hewitt of the Fourth South Carolina Cavalry was informed of the landing. Hewitt jumped on his horse and rode toward Fields Point to ascertain the numbers and movement of the Federals. Hewitt found that the pickets and twenty men with Lieutenant A.E. Gilchrist had fallen back to Arthur Middleton's plantation. Hewitt reported to Green Pond the location of the Federals, who were at that time at Middleton's rice mill. The courier arrived at the Confederate camp at Green Pond at 7:00 a.m. and informed Major Emanuel of the attack.[182]

The *John Adams*, with Montgomery and the rest of his command, including the Third Rhode Island Heavy Artillery, steamed upstream. As they were closing in on Combahee Ferry at around 6:30 a.m., Corporal Wall, chief of the pickets at the ferry, spotted the *Adams*. Wall immediately sent a courier to the main camp eight miles away at Green Pond and, mounting his men on horseback, followed over the pontoon bridge and across the causeway, taking cover in the breastworks at the head of the causeway. The Confederates could already see the smoke from the plantations downriver.[183]

The guns of the *John Adams* fired twice at the fleeing riders as they passed over the mile-wide causeway. Turning, the Confederates saw the *Adams* approach the causeway side of the ferry and land a force. Upon reaching the pontoon bridge over the Combahee, the men on the *Adams* took up the bridge and set it on fire. Captain Hoyt and his men disembarked on the causeway and proceeded across to the far (Colleton) side. Captain Brayton proceeded up the left bank of the river to Middleton's Newport Plantation, where he was to carry out "special orders." These orders included confiscating any and all property and laying waste to what could not be carried off.[184]

Not all the Confederates fled across the causeway. A group of cavalry stationed at Cotton Hope, the Combahee Rangers, were at William Middleton's plantation on the left bank. Confederate lieutenant Brunson noted the *Adams* coming upriver, and he and several of his men quickly saddled their horses. Leaving the rest of his detachment, Brunson rode to Mr. Walter Blake to inform him of the raid. The Federals formed up and advanced across the fields to the house. The thirty to forty men of the Third Rhode Island proceeded to torch the buildings of the plantation, sparing only the brick slave houses. For three to four hours, the Combahee Rangers kept to the woods, observing the Federals and attempting to stop the slaves from reaching the Union ships. While many of the slaves made it to safety, many more were cut off from escape by the Confederates and plantation overseers with dogs.[185] One of the men of the Third Rhode Island later wrote, "This was the saddest sight of the whole expedition—so many soles [*sic*] within sight of freedom, and yet unable to attain it."[186]

Captain Hoyt and the remainder of the men of the Second South Carolina left the *Adams* at the causeway. The *John Adams* then slowly ran up the river for a very short distance until stopped by obstructions and pilings in the river. Turning back, the men tied up the ship at the causeway. Hoyt's men proceeded across the causeway, which was approximately one mile long and sixteen feet wide. The causeway was slightly elevated above the rice fields on either side and afforded no cover to the exposed black troops.

Not a man shirked as they proceeded across. Upon reaching the head of the causeway, they found the Confederates had fallen back farther, some of them riding to the plantation of Mr. C.T. Lowndes on the right and to the plantation of Colonel W.C. Heyward on the left to warn them of the oncoming Federals.[187]

Colonel Heyward was at home on his plantation when the Federals steamed up the Combahee. At 6:15 a.m. on the second, Heyward received a knock on his door from a servant, who reported that the driver of the field hands in the lower rice field had spotted a boat coming up the river. Heyward spied the boat, "a large ferry boat, with the United States flag flying, upper deck crowded with people." Giving an order to take his slaves to the woods, Heyward watched as the boat slowly approached the ferry, the Confederate pickets at the ferry crossing not moving until the boat was within one and one-quarter mile from the ferry. After the pickets crossed the causeway, Heyward asked one of the men why he had waited so long to report. He replied, "Ordered not to report until we are certain of facts—thought they might be our boats." Heyward had been watching the boat for an hour.[188]

Not being satisfied with the response of the pickets, Heyward rode directly to the camp at Green Pond. From Green Pond, Heyward telegraphed Brigadier General W.S. Walker, commander of the Third Military District. Walker immediately ordered the camp at McPhersonville to Green Pond via the railroad to aid Major Emanuel.[189]

Captain W.L. Trenholm responded with three companies of the Eleventh South Carolina Volunteers and two companies of the Rutledge Mounted Riflemen and Horse Artillery—247 men in all. Arriving by train at Green Pond at two o'clock in the afternoon, Trenholm found all of Emanuel's forces out in the field. Not having orders, Trenholm sent some men forward to ascertain what was happening, only to find the action over.[190]

Major Emanuel was notified of the Union ships by courier at seven o'clock in the morning. Emanuel ordered twenty men under Lieutenant Gilchrist to Fields Point. The rest of his command would be ordered to Stokes Causeway, where they would support two pieces of Bowman's Artillery. At Stokes Causeway was a large prepared earthwork. Lieutenant P.L. Breeden was ordered to Colonel Heyward's plantation at the Combahee Ferry causeway. Initially, Captain Godbold had ordered the other two pieces of Bowman's Artillery to Fields Point to support the troops there; however, Major Emanuel, not being familiar with the territory, and fearing the flotilla would soon be trying to reach the railroad bridge over the Salkehatchie (upper Combahee) River, ordered the two pieces to the bridge. This was sixteen miles from Green Pond by a circular route. Emanuel was not aware that the main depot at McPhersonville was only five miles from the bridge and, in effect, had taken his much-needed cannon out of the fight.[191]

The black Union troops advanced across the causeway in double-file regular order. Reaching Heyward's plantation, they fanned out, taking torches to all the buildings except those on the slave street. They plundered the plantation of any property they could carry, including the colonel's finest horse and sword. What they couldn't take, they burned. Exhorted by the soldiers, the slaves streamed across the causeway to freedom and the safety of the *Adams*.[192]

On C.T. Lowndes's plantation, the Union troops couldn't reach the settlement or the main house, as both were protected by a small but deep swamp and there was simply no time to cross. The *Adams* had briefly stopped at Jacks Creek two miles by river from the ferry but only a half mile by land, and a landing party of twenty-five to thirty in small boats came ashore near the rice mill. Lowndes's steam-powered rice mill and all of his barns and stores of rice and cotton were burned. The floodgates here, as downriver, were opened as well, flooding the fields.[193]

At Lowndes's plantation, an overseer by the name of Pipkin attempted to order the slaves to the woods. But the slaves scattered and started running for the boats. Pipkin saw the Confederates coming slowly from the direction of Green Pond. Lieutenant Breeden inquired about the location of any Federals at Lowndes's place. At the corner of the fence to Heyward's plantation, Breeden stopped and conferred with one of the pickets. He then sent six men up a nearby path to the Smith plantation, which was on the north side of Heyward's plantation and not under attack. Moving on another quarter mile, Breeden dismounted his men and sent them to Heyward's place, where they found all the Federals and slaves gone and the plantation buildings in smoky ruins. Breeden and his men moved deliberately down to the breastworks at the head of the causeway. Having completed their tasks at Heyward's plantation, the men of the Second South Carolina Volunteers, with the newly freed slaves in front of them, were down the causeway some three hundred yards when they were fired on by a few of the Confederates under Lieutenant Breeden. The black troops returned fire, and the *Adams* also fired its cannon. The Confederates made a hasty retreat.[194]

Overseer Pipkin asked Lieutenant Breeden for some men to ride with him to the Lowndes place. Lieutenant Breeden gave him two men. Upon approaching the barn compound, they were informed that most of the field hands and the remaining Federal troops were now at the yard. Pipkin rode back and offered to guide Breeden and the rest of his men. Breeden declined the offer, stating that he was under the orders of Major Emanuel and that the major was at the head of the causeway. Pipkin rode to Emanuel and implored him to give him some men; Emanuel gave him six of Breeden's men. Pipkin's frustration grew, as he could not get the men assigned to him to go any faster than a walk. They eventually met a Sergeant Smith at the plantation, who assumed command of the men. By the time they got to where they could leave their horses, they were down to five men, the others having slipped away.

When Pipkin reached the barn, all the Union soldiers and most of the slaves had left and were on their way to the boats. Seeing the fleeing slaves, the infuriated Pipkin wanted to go down the rice field dike and cut them off from the boats. Sergeant Smith warned against it, nothing that Pipkin would receive fire from the boat. Not listening, Pipkin ran down to within 125 yards of the landing, where he spied a group of twenty-five to thirty who had not been taken aboard yet.[195] In front of the group was a single girl. Pipkin ordered her to stop. After she refused his order, Pipkin took aim and shot the girl. She fell, got up and ran back to where the others were. Pipkin took custody of them and herded them back to the plantation yard.[196]

The *John Adams*, with Montgomery and Tubman onboard, left the ferry and slowly descended downriver, having left total destruction on the Heyward, Lowndes and Middleton plantations. Not a building was left standing (except those on the slave streets), the rice fields were in ruins and the trunks for regulating the water had been destroyed. Most of the slaves who could make it to the boats were taken aboard along with large amounts of furniture and livestock.

With the *John Adams* leaving the ferry, Major Emanuel and Lieutenant Breeden met in the yard of the Lowndes place. The major sent an overseer for the Smith plantation as a guide with Lieutenant Breeden with orders to stay close to the river, watching the movements of the gunboats. Emanuel took Pipkin as a guide and headed back to the Stokes Road and down to the causeway.[197]

Before reaching the earthworks at Stokes Causeway, Major Emanuel was informed by a courier that Captain Godbold and Captain Bomar with his two field pieces had advanced toward Middleton's plantation near Tar Bluff. Being notified that the Federals were still at the mill, Emanuel ordered the artillery forward. Before reaching the mill, however, Emanuel was informed that the Federal troops had left. Finding the Union ship just off Middleton Bluff just upriver of Tar Bluff, Emanuel ordered the artillery down to Fields Point in an attempt to cut them off. Taking the road from Tar Bluff to Fields Point, Emanuel found his command surrounded by the men of the Second South Carolina under Captain Thompson. The Confederates were on a short causeway through a swamp. The Second South Carolina was at the edge of the swamp with a clear view of the oncoming Confederates. As Thompson's men opened fire on the Confederates, Emanuel ordered Bomar to bring up and fire his cannon, which he did with little effect. Not knowing the disposition of the Union troops in the swamp, Emanuel and his force fell back to Tar Bluff, where they found Captain Godbold. Godbold stated that he had encountered the same thing and that when his troops attacked, they had been driven back by the guns of the *Weed*.[198]

Captain Apthorp could see the black smoke that signaled the destruction of the plantations upriver. Everywhere the slaves streamed down to the boat until it was filled to capacity. In his papers, titled "Montgomery's Raids in Florida, Georgia, and South Carolina," Apthorp wrote, "Remembering the treatment that these poor people would suffer for their attempt to escape to the Yankees, it was hard to leave them. But it was impossible to take another one, and sadly we swung away from the landing."[199]

The *Adams* came downriver, where it met the *Weed* and stopped to take on additional escaping slaves before finally getting under way. Captain Carver had kept up a running skirmish all day with the Confederates near Middleton's Mill. By the time the *Weed* and *John Adams* reached Tar Bluff, Carver and his men were there waiting. Carver and his men boarded the *Adams*. The *Weed* ran down to check on the safety of Captain Thompson at Fields Point. Having left Thompson and his men with no support, the men on the *Weed* were anxious for their safety. Just as the *Weed* arrived, they spotted Confederate artillery set to fire on the earthworks occupied by Thompson's men at Fields Point. The *Weed* immediately fired on the Confederates, causing them to retreat from the superior Federal firepower.[200]

The two ships, overladen with troops, plunder, livestock and the freed slaves, slowly headed back to Beaufort. At around 5:00 p.m., just as they were leaving the Combahee, the heavens opened up with a thunderstorm. The ships cautiously navigated home on a stormy night, arriving in Beaufort the following morning of the third. For the Federals, the raid was a complete success. The fertile rice fields and plantations of the Combahee were in ruin, and close to 800 men, women and children were freed from bondage, with 150 of the men volunteering to join the Union regiment.

Despite a full day of skirmishing, the only Confederate death was Private James E. Fripp of the Fifth South Carolina Cavalry, who was sick and on leave at his home in Green Pond. Volunteering to guide the Confederates unfamiliar with the area, Fripp was wounded four times and succumbed to his wounds on June 13. No Federals were killed in the raid. At least one slave was killed and numerous others wounded.[201]

There is no official count of the number of slaves who escaped during the raid. Montgomery gave the figure as 727, while Harriet Tubman used the number 756. No matter the number, the Combahee River Raid will be long remembered for the mass freeing of enslaved people by black troops. The men of the Second South Carolina Volunteers showed their bravery, particularly across the mile-wide Combahee causeway. The plans of Saxton and Hunter, along with the expertise and tactics of Montgomery, had delivered to the Union the results it had so long desired.[202]

CHAPTER 8

REACTION

The reaction to the raid was immediate and profound on both sides.
Upon reaching Beaufort, the *John Adams* and the *Harriet A. Weed*
docked at the wharf at the foot of Bay Street. The newly freed slaves were
taken to the Baptist church before heading to a resettlement camp on St.
Helena Island. At the church, the newly freed slaves, along with throngs
of other Beaufort residents, pressed to the steps of the church to hear the
speech of the Union colonel.

Montgomery filed a brief report with Hunter upon returning to Beaufort:

> *General, I have the honor to report that, in obedience with your orders,
> I proceeded up the Combahee River, on the steamers* John Adams
> *and* Harriet A. Weed, *with a detachment of three hundred (300)
> men of the Second South Carolina Volunteer Regiment and a section
> of the Third Rhode Island Battery, commanded by Captain Brayton.
> We ascended the river some twenty-five (25) miles, destroyed a pontoon
> bridge, together with a large amount of cotton and rice, and some other
> property, and brought away seven hundred and twenty seven slaves, and
> some fine horses. We had some sharp skirmishes, in all of which the
> men behaved splendidly.*

General Hunter telegraphed Washington with the news:

HEADQUARTERS DEPARTMENT OF THE SOUTH
Hilton Head, Port Royal, S.C.
June 3, 1863
Hon. E.M. STANTON
Secretary of War, Washington, D.C.

SIR: I have much pleasure in transmitting to you herewith certified copy of a telegraphic report just received from Col. James Montgomery, commanding Second South Carolina Regiment, of the result of the first of a series of raids upon the main-land, now organized and in process of being carried out.

From the report you will see that Colonel Montgomery, with 300 men of his regiment and a section of the Third Rhode Island Battery, commanded by Captain Brayton, penetrated the country of the enemy 25 miles, destroyed a pontoon bridge across the Combahee River, together with a vast amount of cotton, rice, and other property, and brought away with him 725 slaves and some 5 horses.[203]

The *New South*, a newspaper published for the Union troops at Port Royal, reported:

On Monday evening last, five companies of the 2nd S.C. Vols…under the command of Col. Montgomery, started on an expedition which had for it's main objective the recruiting of soldiers for the 2nd S.C. Regiment…After gathering all the troops and taking on board 727 negroes, men, women, children and a few fine horses, the expedition returned to Beaufort.[204]

A Union surgeon who had participated in the raid, Surgeon Robinson, sent in a sketch and reported the action, which was published in the July Fourth edition of *Harper's Weekly*:

I inclose [sic] you a sketch of the operations of Colonel James Montgomery (formerly of Kansas), of the Second South Carolina Volunteers (colored), in the interior of South Carolina, among the rice plantations on the Combahee.

We destroyed a vast amount of rice, corn, and cotton, stored in the barns and rice-mills, with many valuable steam-engines. We broke the sluice-gates and flooded the fields so that the present crop, which was growing beautifully, will be a total loss. We carried out the President's proclamation, too, and brought away about 800 contrabands, 150 of whom are now serving their country in the regiment which liberated them. The rest were old men, women, and children. The rebel loss from our visit must amount to several millions of dollars. We are now about commencing operations on the Georgia coast.

We skirmished all day with the rebels, but escaped without the loss of a man. Their cavalry killed and wounded some of the slaves as they swarmed to the protection of the old flag.[205]

One of the first Northern newspapers to offer an account of the raid was the *Wisconsin State Journal*, which published the article in its June 20 edition. The reporter was evidently on the scene as the troops and freed slaves returned to Beaufort. The article gives some details of the raid and also adds that "the Colonel was followed by a speech from the black woman who led the raid, and under whose inspiration it was originated and conducted." Then, without naming her, the reporter adds, "And now a word of this woman—this black heroine—this fugitive slave. She is now called 'Moses.'"[206]

Following the *Wisconsin State Journal* article, Tubman's old friend Franklin B. Sanborn, editor of the *Commonwealth*, picked up and repeated the *Journal* story, making numerous corrections. In his article, he named Harriet Tubman as the aforementioned woman, and he would go on to publish one of the first biographies of Tubman. While Sanborn certainly had his reasons for publishing and naming Tubman, this could have created a real danger for her. It was common for Confederates to get copies of Northern newspapers. Just prior to the Combahee Raid, a Northern newspaper, the *New York Tribune*, had printed a story about coming raids of which the Confederates were well aware. By naming Harriet Tubman as a leader of the Combahee River Raid, the *Commonwealth* was possibly putting her life in jeopardy, which might have restricted her movements.

Interestingly, despite the credit given her by the Wisconsin paper, Tubman dictated a letter to Sanborn in which she laments, "Don't you think we colored people are entitled to some credit for that exploit, under the lead of the brave Colonel Montgomery?" Her motives for making this statement are unknown. Being illiterate, Tubman couldn't read the newspapers and would not have had access to many of them—certainly not before she wrote to Sanborn. She would have known little about the reaction to the raid in the North. It's possible that after witnessing Montgomery receive much of the credit and a hero's welcome in Beaufort, she thought more credit should be given to her and the black troops of the Second South Carolina. Tubman was never shy about telling her story; however, the letter to Sanborn seems out of character for her.[207]

Naturally, the views of the Confederates were much different from the Union accounts. Following the raid, Confederate general W.S. Walker wrote to General Jordan, "The enemy burned four fine residences and six mills, and took off with them about 700 negroes, who are believed to have gone with great alacrity and to some extent with pre-conceived arrangement." With this statement, Walker was already trying to shift some of the blame for the raid. Later authors would explicate on this and suggest that the slaves had been informed of the raid. However, in numerous instances, the accounts of the participants state that the workers in the fields initially took to the woods before finally fleeing to the boats.[208]

In her journal, Meta Morris Grimball of St. John's Berkeley wrote, "There has been a very destructive Raid on Combahee. Millions of property destroyed & carried off; 6 or 7 hundred negroes by 200 armed negroes with white Officers."[209]

Catherine Heyward of the Heyward family wrote to Sophia and Mary Clinch a few days later. In her June 5 letter, she remarked: "The last news from the Combahee River in S.C. is rather startling to the family here. The Yankees have devastated the plantations, six or seven of them, by their raid the other day, carrying off six or seven hundred negroes. Mr. William C. Heyward, whose mother is the old lady in New York, it is supposed ruined, and Mr. Charles Lowndes and Mr. [Walter] Blake are the next great sufferers."[210]

The *Charleston Mercury* published two articles on the raid, one of which follows:

The Enemy Raid on the Banks of the Combahee

We have gathered some additional particulars of the recent destructive Yankee raid along the banks of the Combahee. The latest official despatch [sic] from Gen. WALKER, dated Green Pond, eleven o'clock Tuesday night, and which was received here on Wednesday morning, conveyed intelligence that the enemy had entirely disappeared.

It seems that the first landing of the Vandals, whose force consisted mainly of three [black] companies, officered by whites, took place at Field Point, on the plantation of Dr. R.L. BAKER, at the mouth of the Combahee River. After destroying the residence and outbuildings, the incendiaries proceeded along the river bank, visiting successively the plantations of Mr. OLIVER MIDDLETON, Mr. ANDREW W. BURNETT, Mr. WM. KIRKLAND, Mr. JOSHUA NICHOLLS, Mr. JAMES PAUL, Mr. MANIGAULT, Mr. CHAS. T. LOWNDES and Mr. WM. C. HEYWARD. After pillaging the premises of these gentlemen, the enemy set fire to the residences, outbuildings and whatever grain, etc., they could find. The last place at which they stopped was the plantation of WM. C. HEYWARD, and, after their work of devastation there had been consummated, they destroyed the pontoon bridge at Combahee Ferry. They then drew off, taking with them between 600 and 700 negros [sic], belonging chiefly, as we are informed, to Mr. WM. C. HEYWARD and Mr. C.T. LOWNDES.

The residences on these plantations are located at distances from the river, varying in different cases from one to two miles. On the plantation of Mr. NICHOLLS between 8,000 and 10,000 bushels of rice were destroyed. Besides his residence and outbuildings, which were burned, he lost a choice library of rare books, valued at $10,000. Several overseers are missing, and it is supposed that they are in the hands of the enemy.

The success of a marauding expedition of this character is certainly a very mortifying circumstance. We are informed that Tar Bluff, down the river, below the plantation of Mr. BURNETT, commands the Combahee, and that a few well served guns at that point would prevent gunboats from going up the river. And in like manner it has been suggested that a few guns, skillfully managed, if placed at Chapman's Fort, on the Ashepoo River, would prevent any ascent of the stream. It is a matter of regret the troops recently stationed between the Combahee and the Ashepoo are ignorant of the localities and roads in an important region, in which it is so difficult to give warning of the enemy approach, and where rapidity of movement is so important an element of military success.

Confederate captain John F. Lay investigated the action. In a seething report, he sought to both blame the Confederate troops and to speculate that there might have been outside help, possibly to deflect some of the blame from the inadequate Confederate troops. Previous to the raid and his transfer to Green Pond, Major Emmanuel had been cited in the Georgetown District for the lack of discipline and military bearing of the men under his command. He seems to have been deficient in his military duties.

This raid by a mixed party of blacks and degraded whites seems to have been designed only for plunder, robbery, and destruction of private property;

85

in carrying it out they have disregarded all rules of civilized war, and have acted more as fiends than human beings. Fortunately the planters had removed their families, who thus avoided outrage and insult. The enemy seem to have been well posted as to the character and capacity of our troops and their small chance of encountering opposition, and to have been well guided by persons thoroughly acquainted with the river and the country. Their success was complete, as evidenced by the total destruction of four fine residences, six valuable mills, with many valuable out-buildings (the residence of Mr. Charles Lowndes alone escaped), and large quantities of rice. They also successfully carried off from 700 to 800 slaves of every age and sex. These slaves, it is believed, were invited by these raiders to join them in their fiendish work of destruction. The loss of Messrs. Nickols [sic] and Kirkland was very great—an entire loss, including for the former a large and choice library, valued at $15,000.[211]

Lieutenant Colonel Fremantle of the British Coldstream Guards toured the South in the spring and early summer of 1863. While in Charleston twelve days after the raid he met with Walter Blake, one of the planters on the Combahee:

Mr. Walter Blake arrived soon after dinner; he had come up from his plantation on the Combahee River on purpose to see me. He described the results of the late Yankee raid up that river: forty armed negroes and a few whites in a miserable steamer were able to destroy and burn an incalculable amount of property, and carry off hundreds of negroes. Mr. Blake got off very cheap, having only lost twenty-four this time, but he only saved the remainder by his own personal exertions and determination. He had now sent all his young males two hundred miles into the interior for greater safety. He seemed to have a very rough time of it, living all alone in that pestilential climate. A neighbouring planter, Mr. Lowndes, had lost 290 negroes, and a Mr. Kirkland was totally ruined.[212]

Joshua Nicholls watched as his plantation and those of his neighbors were looted and burned. In an article in the *Charleston Mercury*, he described the scene:

They came up to my house, and in a very short time it was set on fire. I looked towards Mr. Kirkland's place, and soon perceived the smoke rising from the direction of his residence. Presently the mill, overseer house and stables on his place, also the threshing mill and barns upon my own place, as well as those upon Mr. Lowndes and Col. Heyward, were burning almost simultaneously. The negros, men and women, were rushing to the boat with their children, now and then greeting some one whom they recognized among the uniformed negros, and who were probably former runaways from the various plantations in the neighborhood. The negros seemed to be utterly transformed, drunk with excitement, and capable of the wildest excesses. The roaring of the flames, the barbarous howls of the negros, the blowing of horns, the harsh steam whistle, and the towering columns of smoke from every quarter, made an impression on my mind which can never be effaced. [213]

Initially, the Union generals and Northern newspapers were elated and described Montgomery and his raid in glowing terms. Soon, however, they were forced to retreat from this position. There was outrage in the Charleston papers and complaints from General Beauregard concerning the conduct of Montgomery and his men. To the Confederates, the burning and looting of private residences was an outrage and against the doctrine of civilized warfare.

Even some of Hunter's own officers had distain for Montgomery's tactics. Colonel Thomas W. Higginson wrote, "Montgomery has been a sore disappointment to me and to General Saxton, with whom he is at sword's point. I should have such hard work to coerce him into my notions of civilized warfare." Of curious note is the fact that although Higginson had much distain for Montgomery's tactics, he was a staunch supporter of and an instigator for John Brown and his raid on Harpers Ferry. [214] In a letter to Louisa Higginson just after the raid, Higginson wrote, "Montgomery's raids are dashing but his brigand practices I detest & condemn—they will injure these people [black soldiers] & make a reaction at the North." [215]

Robert Gould Shaw, colonel of the Fifty-fourth Massachusetts, arrived in Beaufort the same day Montgomery returned from the Combahee Raid. Shaw wrote to Massachusetts governor John Andrew about his arrival and remarked about Montgomery's "Indian style of fighting" and his tactics, adding that "bushwhacking seems pretty small potatoes." He later wrote:

Montgomery, who seems the only active man in this Department, is enormously energetic, and devoted to the cause, but he is a bush-whacker in his fighting, and a perfect fanatic in other respects. He never drinks, smokes, or swears, & considers that praying, shooting, burning & hanging are the true means to put down the Rebellion. If he had been educated as a military man in rather a different school, I think he would accomplish a great deal, & he may yet in a certain way…I never met a man who impressed me as being more conscientious.[216]

In a letter home to his mother, Shaw wrote, "The bushwacker Montgomery is a strange compound. He allows no swearing or drinking & is anti tobacco—But he burns and destroys wherever he goes with great gusto, & looks as if he had quite a taste for hanging people and throat-cutting whenever a suitable subject offers."[217]

The backlash against Montgomery's tactics and scorched-earth policy was such that just one week later, on June 9, Major General Hunter issued instructions (including General Order No. 100) on the proper conduct of war to Montgomery. Hunter reminded Montgomery that certain items that could be used by the enemy were fair game, that he was to give protection to any "fugitives" and that he was to immediately enroll and arm any able-bodied men as soldiers. Exempt from destruction were crops in the field. Hunter went on to write, "This right of war, though unquestionable in certain extreme cases, is not to be lightly used, and if wantonly used might fall under that part of the instructions which prohibits devastation. All household furniture, libraries, churches and hospitals you will of course spare."[218]

A week later, two days after the admonishment of Hunter and General Order No. 100, Shaw would learn firsthand about the tactics of Montgomery and his distain for Southerners and their property when Montgomery and Shaw led their troops to Darien, Georgia, plundering and burning the undefended, deserted town. After this incident, Confederate general Beauregard even went so far as to equate the tactics of Montgomery and Hunter with those of Britain's burning of Havre de Grace in the War of 1812. In a letter to General Quincy Gillmore, Hunter's successor, Beauregard summed up his feelings: "In conclusion, it is my duty to inquire whether the acts which resulted in the burning of the defenseless villages of Darien and Bluffton, and the ravages on the Combahee, are regarded by you as legitimate measures of war, which you will feel authorized to resort to hereafter."[219]

The area of the Combahee was devastated. Crops were ruined; mills, farm buildings and homes burned to the ground; and fields destroyed. Livestock and personal property were taken or burned. The rice fields of the Combahee, some of the most productive agricultural lands in South Carolina, were in ruins. This was a war not on the army of the Confederacy but on the slaveholders, an outgrowth of the philosophy Montgomery shared with John Brown and honed in the bloody, rolling hills of Kansas.

Chapter 9

MYTH AND REALITY

Harriet Tubman was little known outside of abolitionist circles until Franklin B. Sanborn published a lengthy article about her in his newspaper, the *Commonwealth*. Prior to this, Tubman had been known only for her exploits in rescuing slaves from Maryland. But the Combahee River Raid changed that. Sanborn changed the narrative to suit his needs, creating a figure that is based more on conjecture than fact. Sanborn didn't have any firsthand knowledge of the raid; he merely picked up the story.

Tubman had already achieved an almost mythical status in certain circles before the war. By publishing her biography in the *Commonwealth* in July 1863, Sanborn reached a wider audience and cemented her place in American and African American history.

Tubman was known throughout abolitionist circles for her storytelling ability. She was a frequent speaker at meetings, where she would enthrall her audiences with her tales of escaping slavery and her many trips back to the Eastern Shore. At the same time, the abolitionist movement needed Tubman to put a face to slavery and the risks in escaping. She justified their philosophy and their cause.

We know from Bradford's books and numerous sources much of Tubman's wartime duties and activities. She is mentioned numerous times by those who knew her in South Carolina. In addition, after the war, she fought for many years for a pension and back pay from the federal government. For this reason, Charles P. Wood, an attorney from Auburn, New York, compiled all of her papers and sought the testimony of many who knew her and her activities during the war. We draw on these sources for much of what we know about Tubman. However, we need to carefully examine some of these sources being used to bolster her pension application.

Even though Bradford's books are poorly written and there are many inaccuracies, they are the only primary sources of Tubman's involvement in the raid other than the problematic *Wisconsin State Journal* account. Tubman is not mentioned in the *Official Records*, nor is she mentioned in the diaries and journals of her contemporaries who participated in the raid or were in Port Royal at the time. Captain Apthorp, the commander stationed on the *Harriet A. Weed* during the raid, never mentioned her. Nor did Hunter, Montgomery, Saxton or even her old friend Higginson. So, if Tubman was such an integral part of the raid, as some writers would lead us to believe, why did they not mention her?

In 1943, author Earl Conrad published his book *Harriet Tubman: Negro Soldier and Abolitionist*, in which he refers to the *Commonwealth* and *Wisconsin State Journal* stories, Bradford's biography and fictionalized children's books. Conrad makes assertions that were unsubstantiated and yet are being picked up and expanded by authors even today. Although it is the most repeated, the Combahee Raid is one of the most poorly documented and exaggerated periods in Tubman's life.[220]

In his book, Conrad gives Tubman credit for the formulation of the raid and claims that Montgomery was the second in command to Tubman. He makes this deduction in part from the *Wisconsin State Journal* newspaper account. Conrad obviously had little knowledge of Montgomery's background and basic military protocol. Milton Sernett, in his book *Harriet Tubman: Myth, Memory and History*, notes that Conrad wrote an article for the *Negro World Digest* in which he stated, "But the Combahee raid is significant as the only military engagement in American history wherein a woman, black or white, led." A more modern variation of the quote has since emerged, often attributed to General Saxton: "This is the only military command in American history wherein a woman, black or white, led the raid and under whose inspiration it was originated and conducted." Yet this, too, has no basis in fact, and as one Tubman scholar wrote, "It sounds like something picked up from one of those many poorly researched essays on Tubman that get inflated on the Internet."[221]

The websites of both the Smithsonian Institute and the CIA repeat this claim. The Smithsonian site states:

Tubman became the first woman in the country's history to lead a military expedition when she helped Col. James Montgomery plan a night raid to free slaves from rice plantations along the Combahee River. On June 1, 1863, Montgomery, Tubman and several hundred black soldiers traveled up the river in gunboats, avoiding remotely detonated mines that had been placed along the waterway. When they reached the shore, they destroyed a Confederate supply depot and freed more than 750 slaves…During the Civil War, Tubman served with the Union Army as a rifle-toting scout and spy. In June 1863, she helped lead a gunboat raid on plantations along the Combahee River near Beaufort, South Carolina, an action that freed more than 700 slaves.[222]

This is a problem on a number of levels. Tubman did not lead the raid, and there is no documentary evidence that she had a hand in planning the raid. There is no evidence that there were "remotely detonated mines," and there was no Confederate supply depot for the Union troops to destroy. So how could so many mistakes be written in one paragraph from one of the leading institutions in the country?

In 2009, the CIA published *Intelligence in the American Civil War*, a fifty-page book by Thomas Allen that repeats many of these same false assertions. Allen wrote, "Reporting on the raid to Secretary of War Stanton, Brigadier General Rufus Saxton said, 'This is the only military command in American history wherein a woman, black or white, led the raid, and under whose inspiration it was originated and conducted.'" He then added, "He [Montgomery] made her his second-in-command for the night raid up the Combahee River that freed more than 750 plantation slaves."[223]

Many of these assertions have now been accepted as fact and are part of the mythology that has grown around Tubman. For example, in a 2005 Internet article for Discovery News concerning the Highway 17 road project, Jennifer Viegas quoted a historian who further propagated these claims:

"This was the first time in United States history that a woman planned and executed an armed military action," said Edward Salo, a historian with Brockington and Associates Inc. who has been working on the project. "Her intelligence gave the Union troops critical details about the location of Confederate forces. Before this time, the Union forces had little information about the location and strength of Confederate troops," he said. Salo said that, before the raid, a disguised Tubman visited slaves at South Carolina plantations and instructed them that

Union ships would be near the ferry crossing on the night of June 2, 1863. Whistles blowing from the ships would be the signal for them to run toward the vessels to their freedom.

Again, what is most disturbing is the fact that these assertions are completely unfounded and can't be substantiated by any documentary evidence.

The Combahee River Raid was an outgrowth of the military tactics used by James Montgomery in the 1850s, the time of Bleeding Kansas. Major General David Hunter was Montgomery's superior officer when Montgomery was with Senator Lane at the beginning of the war. Hunter was well aware of the tactics Montgomery used in Kansas and seems to have wholeheartedly approved of the same tactics in South Carolina. The Combahee River Raid was a clear example of the military philosophy Montgomery and Hunter had used prior to and during the early days of the war. This was evident in successive raids like the one on Darien a little over a week later, a raid Tubman did not participate in, as she was in Beaufort at the time.

From the beginning in the Department of the South, General Hunter had problems filling his regiments with black troops. He resorted to conscription, a method opposed by both the newly freed blacks and the superintendents on the plantations, who needed the men to work the cotton. When Montgomery arrived in South Carolina, he was a commander without any troops. He had to go to Key West, Florida, to raise his first 150 men. Hunter and Montgomery planned a number of raids, patterned after the early raids in Florida, to drive quickly into the interior, disrupt the plantations and commerce, destroy the slaveholders' property and, most importantly, use their slaves to fill the regiment. Captain Apthorp of the Second South Carolina Volunteers, one of the commanders on the raid, gives this as the main reason for the expedition: "This raid was simply to help fill up our regiment and give our men a relish for the work that we were to do all along the Southern coast."[224]

In his brief report to Secretary of War Stanton on June 3, 1863, Hunter wrote, "Colonel Montgomery with his forces will repeat his incursions as rapidly as possible in different directions, injuring the enemy all he can and carrying away his slaves, thus rapidly filling up the South Carolina regiments in the department, of which there are now four."[225]

It is obvious that this raid was to be just the first in a series of such raids. This brings into question the leadership of the raid. In his biography of Tubman, Conrad makes a number of assumptions, ignoring the *Official*

Records and even the narrative in Bradford's book, which Tubman had dictated to her. Bradford wrote, "General Hunter asked her at one time if she would go with several gunboats up the Combahee River…Tubman said she would go if Colonel Montgomery was to be appointed commander of the expedition. Accordingly, Colonel Montgomery was appointed to the command, and Harriet, with several men under her, the principal of whom was J. Plowden, who's [*sic*] pass I have, accompanied the expedition."[226]

Nowhere in Bradford's account is Tubman mentioned as having a leadership role—contrarily, Tubman gives Montgomery the leadership role. Nor is there any indication that Tubman did any spying in the area prior to the raid. Two "scouts" on the raid were Samuel Heyward and Charles Simmons, both of whom were from the area and acted as pilots. Another scout mentioned prominently is Walter D. Plowden. Plowden, originally with the Thirteenth New York Militia for three months, was a servant to the surgeon. With the surgeon leaving, Plowden became a scout for General Hunter. The *Congressional Globe*, a paper that reported congressional news, gives a fair accounting of Plowden's role in the Department of the South. As far as the Combahee Raid, Plowden is said to have scouted up the Combahee at night with eight colored men, being gone for five days. Tubman is not mentioned. Immediately after returning, Plowden accompanied Montgomery on the Combahee Raid. Again, there is no mention of Tubman. It is interesting to note that some facts seem to have been mixed up in the *Congressional Globe* account. Regardless, it does assign the role of scout for the Combahee expedition to Plowden.[227]

In Plowden's pension application, there are numerous scouting forays reported with number of men and location. In her pension application and documents, Tubman gives no indication of her scouting activities other than some endorsements. Plowden was awarded back pay in the amount of $1,000. Tubman's pension as a scout and/or spy and back pay were denied. Tubman eventually did receive a pension of $12 per month for her nursing duties. There are no documents that detail her role in the Combahee River Raid. That does not mean she did not participate—it only means there is no documentary evidence of her role. In Plowden's pension application, he details numerous forays into enemy territory, as well as the fifteen months he spent in a Confederate prison. In Tubman's pension application, there are no details regarding her involvement as a spy other than accompanying Union troops. It could be this lack of evidence that caused her pension to be denied.

Both Colonel Shaw of the Fifty-fourth Massachusetts, who arrived in Beaufort the day Montgomery returned, and Higginson, the commanding officer of the First South Carolina, briefly describe the raid in letters. They both discuss Montgomery's tactics and the fact that they disagree with them. They do not discuss Tubman in connection with the Combahee River Raid. Furthermore, Tubman is not mentioned in the accounts of Captain Apthorp, General Hunter or General Saxton.

When the initial story came out in the *Wisconsin State Journal*, the reporter included one sentence that has done more to bolster the myth than any other—and this without even naming Tubman: "The Colonel was followed by a speech from the black woman who led the raid, and under whose inspiration it was originated and conducted." Both Sanborn in 1863 and then Conrad in 1943 used this as the basis for their claims of Tubman's leadership of the expedition. The basis for the *Journal's* reporter making this claim might have been revealed in Tubman's dictated letter in which she laments, "Don't you think we colored people are entitled to some credit for that exploit, under the lead of the brave Colonel Montgomery?" Here in this one sentence, she asserts who was the leader of the expedition and why the *Journal* reporter might have credited her with the role as the raid's leader. The more plausible account is that Tubman might have tried to explain to the reporter the role she and her scouts played in the raid, as well as the actions of the Second South Carolina Volunteers. The reporter obviously did not know Tubman, so there were inaccuracies in his report. Troubling is the demeanor of Tubman at this time. Instead of showing joy at the rescue, she shows bitterness for not getting credit for herself or the black troops.[228]

Cynthia Porcher writes in her paper "Harriet Tubman Analysis," "It is likely that Tubman led some kind of jubilation in the church following the raids, but the extent of her involvement in the raids is unclear at best, and the existing primary source information currently available comes from fervent supporters of the abolition movement."[229]

As Sernett wrote in *Harriet Tubman*, "What many Tubman enthusiasts have cited as primary evidence turns out on close inspection to be material compromised by efforts to eulogize Tubman." We might never truly know the full involvement of Tubman in the Combahee River Raid; in this case, the myth has outgrown the reality.

To understand the raid and the obstacles Tubman would have faced, we need to look briefly at the land and the military positions of the Confederates. The area between Union-occupied territory and the Confederate-held mainland was a system of vast, flat salt marshes. Composed of a quicksand-like mud the locals call "pluff mud," these marshes are almost impossible to transverse on foot and too shallow for a vessel. Transecting these salt marshes are numerous smaller streams along with a number of fast-flowing tidal rivers emptying into St. Helena Sound. The only way to approach the area of the raid would be either a very circular route through Confederate-held territory or by boat. The first landing was Fields Point. Fields Point was garrisoned during the late fall through the spring by Confederates backed up by field artillery. For visibility, a large blockhouse was erected on a raised earthen platform, giving an unobstructed view in all directions. Additional picket posts and batteries were stationed up and down the river. Thus, even getting to the mainland would have been extremely difficult and hazardous. The landing is located at the base of where the Confederate camp was situated.

There was only one road leading up the Chehaw Neck, as the area was known. Known as Stocks Road, it led up to the main road, now U.S. Highway 17. The farther north they went on Stocks Road, the farther it led away from the river. When the road was parallel to Combahee Ferry at the main road, it was about six miles from the ferry. In order to scout the area, Tubman would have had to walk from plantation to plantation in an area that was under military control and the watchful eyes of the overseers. This would have been an almost impossible feat even for someone like Tubman, as she was a stranger with no contacts and who didn't understand the native Gullah language. Additionally, even if she were able to scout by land, she would not be able to scout the river. Plowden stated that when he scouted the river, he had gone with eight other men in a rowboat. Even this account could be considered questionable due to the defenses along the river.[230]

There are no accounts of Tubman scouting the Combahee prior to the raid. The only account of scouting immediately before the raid is the testimony from Walter Plowden in his pension application before Congress. Earlier in 1862, an area just south of the ferry had been scouted by a detachment of Union soldiers. However, due to the fortifications and Confederates on station, the Union soldiers could not get to the ferry crossing. This does not mean Tubman never worked as a scout, merely that it is unlikely she did on this occasion. It is probable that Tubman accompanied the Federals on numerous other expeditions, leading to the reporting of her work behind enemy lines. From her accounts, we know she accompanied the troops to Florida as well as on the Combahee Raid.[231]

It was common for civilians and women to accompany the troops on these expeditions. Even on expeditions behind enemy lines they would have acted in numerous capacities, including as nurses. Most of the female nurses for the black troops were, themselves, black. While Tubman might have been included on other raids, she repeats only her account of the Combahee Raid and being on Morris Island when the Federals attacked Battery Wagner.[232]

In reading Bradford's account, we find some of Tubman's descriptions of the damage done to be inaccurate as well. Bradford writes of the raid, "The masters fled; houses and barns and railroad bridges were burned, tracks taken up, torpedoes destroyed, and the object of the expedition fully accomplished." Yet Montgomery and his troops did not get within three miles of the Charleston and Savannah Railroad, and no tracks were taken up. In an article in the *Charleston Mercury*, it was stated that some passengers on the train observed the smoke of the burning plantations as they passed the area. The only bridge burned was the pontoon bridge over the river at the ferry crossing. The railroad bridge over the Combahee was not reached until General W.T. Sherman invaded the state in 1865.

What has gone relatively unnoticed is the role Tubman played in garnering information from the various scouts and the contrabands flooding to the Union lines. Tubman was in a unique position, particularly for a black woman, during the war. Tubman had the ear of the Union generals and officers, as well as the confidence of the blacks in the district. Tubman knew Montgomery as one of John Brown's men. She knew of him, and he knew of her, although they did not meet until the war in South Carolina. Likewise, she came recommended by Governor Andrew and was known by General Hunter. It is not known if General Saxton knew Tubman before the war; however, she would have had his confidence. Tubman was also close with Thomas Wentworth Higginson, the colonel of the First South Carolina Volunteers, and visited him in camp. This friendship stretched back years to before the war and allowed Harriet access to the highest-ranking and most influential officers in the Department of the South.

As for the contrabands, it is inconceivable that an escapee from the plantations would have—or even seek—access to the Union officers. As they crossed the dividing line between the Confederates and the Federals, the contrabands many times would be told to seek out Tubman and inform her of Confederate troop movements or any other pertinent information. Lieutenant George Garrison, posted to one of the Northern-raised black regiments, said, "She has made it a business to see all contrabands escaping from the rebels, and is able to get more intelligence from them than anybody else." This was probably how the Federals knew to strike after the Confederates had pulled back their main body of troops to Green Pond on account of the sickly season. Tubman also had access to locals who worked as scouts and pilots for the various expeditions, again bringing forth valuable information. Tubman wasn't a mere spy but rather, by her own admission, the head of a group of scouts. This is substantiated in her own accounts and by others in her petition for a pension. According to the Charles P. Wood manuscript:

> *Among the original papers in Harriet's possession is a list of the names of the Scouts and Pilots: "Issac Hayward," "Gabriel Cahern," "Geo Chisholm," "Peter Burns," "Mott Blake," "Sandy Sellus"* [and] *"Solomon Gregory." Pilots who know the channels of the River in this vicinity, and who acted as such for Col. Montgomery up the Combahee River: "Chas Simmons"* [and] *"Saml Hayward."*

In addition, there has been found a receipt made out to Tubman on Folly Island in the amount of $100 for "Secret Service" work. This would have been used to pay her scouts and informants.[233]

From the petition submitted by Charles Wood for Tubman's pension, we know the identities of the scouts on the raid: Heyward and Simmons. From Bradford's book and Plowden's *Congressional* account, we know that Plowden was also on the raid. From Plowden's pension bill, we also know that he, along with eight other men, scouted the Combahee prior to the raid. In Bradford's account and the affidavit for Tubman's pension, Tubman was noted as a commander of scouts. Tubman herself did not admit to spying in the interior. Her role as a spy scouting through the Lowcountry, armed with a musket (as shown in Bradford's book to portray her militancy), is

Military commission that tried and convicted the Lincoln conspirators. David Hunter served on the commission. *Library of Congress.*

implausible at best. One author even goes so far as to describe the musket as a sharpshooter's rifle.[234]

With the myths and stories that have grown with each retelling of her story, the narrative of Tubman's role as commander of scouts and as an intermediary to the Union officers places her into another and more proper spotlight that hasn't been acknowledged.

The courage of the Second South Carolina Volunteers has never been recognized. The Second was later reorganized into the Thirty-fourth United States Colored Troops (USCT). The regiment went on to distinguish itself at the Battle of Olustee, and one of its men was awarded the Medal of Honor for saving lives in the sinking of the *Boston* in the Ashepoo River in 1864.

James Montgomery resigned and in late 1864 returned to Kansas, where he became the colonel of the Sixth Kansas State Militia.

Major General David Hunter was reassigned immediately after the Combahee River Raid, although the reassignment had nothing to do with the raid.

General Rufus Saxton finished the war in the Department of the South and became the assistant commissioner of the Freedman's Bureau after the war.

Harriet Tubman stayed in the Department of the South until early 1865, when she returned home to Auburn. She finished out the war nursing at Fort Monroe in Virginia.

The Combahee River plantations were never completely rebuilt. The land lay fallow until after the war. Attempts were made during Reconstruction to farm the rice fields. Hostility between the blacks and the white landowners culminated in the Combahee River Riots and the rise of Wade Hampton to governor. Many of the plantations had to be reclaimed from the United States, having been confiscated as abandoned property by the decree of General W.T. Sherman in 1865. The last rice was grown on Middleton's Newport Plantation about 1914. Since that time, the plantations have been consolidated and are used primarily for hunting and timber farming.

Opposite, top: Historical marker at Combahee River. *Photo by Jeff W. Grigg.*

Opposite, bottom: Reverse of historical marker at Combahee River. *Photo by Jeff W. Grigg.*

DOCUMENTS

F ollowing are documents referenced in the text that, while too large for the body of the work, should be read in their entirety.

REGARDING THE QUESTION OF GENERAL HUNTER RAISING REGIMENTS OF BLACKS:

Resolution adopted by the House of Representatives June 9, 1862.

Resolved, That the Secretary of War be directed to inform this House if General Hunter of the Department of South Carolina has organized a regiment of South Carolina volunteers for the defense of the Union composed of black men (fugitive slaves) and appointed the colonel and other officers to command them.

Second. Was he authorized by the Department to organize and muster into the Army of the United States as soldiers the fugitive or captive slaves?

Third. Has he been furnished with clothing, uniforms, &c., for such force?

Fourth. Has he been furnished by order of the Department of War with arms to be placed in the hands of these slaves?

Fifth. To report any orders given said Hunter and correspondence between him and the Department.

Response from Secretary of War Edwin Stanton

WAR DEPARTMENT
Washington, June 14, 1862
Hon. GALUSHA A. GROW
Speaker of the House of Representatives
SIR: I have the honor to inform the House—

1. That this Department has no official information whether General Hunter, of the Department of the South, has or has not organized a regiment of South Carolina Volunteers for the defense of the Union composed of black men—fugitive slaves—and appointed the colonel and other officers to command them. In order to ascertain whether he has done so or not a copy of the House resolution has been transmitted to General Hunter with instructions to make immediate report thereon.

2. General Hunter was not authorized by the Department to organize and muster into the Army of the United States the fugitive or captive slaves.

3. General Hunter upon his requisition as commander of the [Department of the] South has been furnished with clothing and arms for the force under his command without instructions as to how they should be used.

4. He has not been furnished by order of the Department of War with arms to be placed in the hands of these slaves.

5. In respect to so much of said resolution as directs the Secretary to report, to the House any orders given said Hunter, and correspondence between him and the Department, the President instructs me to answer that the report at this time of the orders given to and correspondence between General Hunter and this Department would, in his opinion, be improper and incompatible with the public welfare.

Very respectfully, your obedient servant,

EDWIN M. STANTON,
Secretary of War.

APPENDIX

Response from General Hunter

HEADQUARTERS DEPARTMENT OF THE SOUTH
Port Royal, S.C., June 23, 1862
Hon. EDWIN M. STANTON
Secretary of War, Washington, D.C.

SIR: I have the honor to acknowledge the receipt of a communication from the Adjutant-General of the Army, dated June 13, 1862, requesting me to furnish you with the information necessary to answer certain resolutions introduced in the House of Representatives on June 9, 1862, on motion of the Hon. Mr. Wickliffe, of Kentucky, their substance being to inquire:

1. Whether I had organized or was organizing a regiment of fugitive slaves in this department?

2. Whether any authority had been given to me from the War Department for such organization; and

3. Whether I had been furnished by the War Department with clothing, uniforms, arms, equipments, etc., for such a force?

Only having received the letter covering these inquiries at a late hour on Saturday night I urge forward my answer in time for the steamer sailing to-day (Monday), this haste preventing me from entering as minutely as I could wish upon many points of detail such as the paramount importance of the subject calls for. But in view of the near termination of the present session of Congress and the widespread interest which must have been awakened by Mr. Wickliffe's resolutions I prefer sending even this imperfect answer to waiting the period necessary for the collection of fuller and more comprehensive data.

To the first question therefore I reply that no regiment of fugitive slaves has been or is being organized in this department. There is however a fine regiment of persons whose late masters are fugitive rebels, men who everywhere fly before the appearance of the national flag, leaving their servants behind them to shift as best they can for themselves. So far indeed are the loyal persons composing this regiment from seeking to avoid the presence of their late owners that they are now one and all working with remarkable industry to place themselves in a position to go in full and effective pursuit of their fugacious and traitorous proprietors.

To the second question I have the honor to answer that the instructions given to Brig. Gen. T.W. Sherman by the Hon. Simon Cameron, late Secretary of War, and turned over to me by succession for my guidance do distinctly authorize me to employ all loyal persons offering their services in defense of the Union and for the suppression of this rebellion in any manner I might see fit or that the circumstances might call for. There is no restriction as to the character or color of the persons to be employed or the nature of the employment—whether civil or military—in which their services should be used. I conclude therefore that I have been authorized to enlist fugitive slaves as soldiers could any such be found in this department. No such characters however have yet appeared within view of our most advanced pickets—the loyal slaves everywhere remaining on their plantations to welcome us, aid us and supply us with food, labor and information. It is the masters who have in every instance been the fugitives, running away from loyal slaves and loyal soldiers and whom we have only partially been able to see—chiefly their heads over ramparts or rifle in hand dodging behind trees in the extreme distance. In the absence of any fugitive-master law the deserted slaves would be wholly without remedy had not the crime of treason given them the right to pursue, capture and bring back those persons of whose protection they have been thus suddenly bereft.

To the third interrogatory it is my painful duty to reply that I never have received any specific authority for issues of clothing, uniforms, arms, equipments and so forth to the troops in question. My general instructions from Mr. Cameron to employ them in any manner I might find necessary, and the military exigencies of the department and the country being my only but in my judgment sufficient justification.

Neither have I had any specific authority for supplying these persons with shovels, spades and pickaxes when employing them as laborers, nor with boats and oars when using them as lightermen; but these are not points included in Mr. Wickliffe's resolution. To me it seemed that liberty to employ men in any particular capacity implied with it liberty also to supply them with the necessary tools, and acting upon this faith I have clothed, equipped and armed the only loyal regiment yet raised in South Carolina.

I must say, in vindication of my own conduct, that had it not been for the many other diversified and imperative claims on my time and attention a much more satisfactory result might have been hoped for, and that in place of only one, as at present, at least five or six well-drilled, brave and thoroughly-acclimated regiments should by this time have been added to the loyal forces of the Union. The experiment of arming the blacks, so far as I have made it, has been a complete and even marvelous success. They are sober, docile, attentive and enthusiastic, displaying great natural capabilities for acquiring the duties of the soldier. They are eager beyond all things to take the field and be led into action, and it is the unanimous opinion of the officers who have had charge of them that in the peculiarities of this climate and country they will prove invaluable auxiliaries, fully equal to the similar regiments so long and successfully used by the British authorities in the West India islands.

In conclusion I would say it is my hope—there appearing no possibility of other re-enforcements, owing to the exigencies of the campaign in the Peninsula—to have organized by the end of next fall, and to be able to present to the Government, from 48,000 to 50,000 of these hardy and devoted soldiers.

Trusting that this letter may form part of your answer to Mr. Wickliffe's resolutions,

I have the honor to be, most respectfully, your obedient servant,

D. HUNTER,
Major-General Commanding

CONFEDERATE AFTER-ACTION REPORT OF THE COMBAHEE RIVER RAID

Extract from inspection report of Colonel John F. Lay, inspector of cavalry, February 2, 1863

HEADQUARTERS THIRD MILITARY DISTRICT,
McPhersonville, May 19, 1863.
Maj. W.P. EMANUEL, Commanding at Green Pond:

MAJOR: The brigadier-general commanding directs me to say that you will require the officers of your detachment to familiarize themselves with the localities and lines of defense in the district of country under your command, a map of which will be sent to you.
Very respectfully, your obedient servant,

JAMES LOWNDES,
Acting Assistant Adjutant-General.

CIRCULAR
HEADQUARTERS THIRD MIL. DIST.,
McPhersonville, May 29, 1863.

Your attention is respectfully called to the following extract from a late Yankee paper:
The New York Tribune *says that the negro troops at Hilton Head, S.C., will soon start upon an expedition, under the command of Colonel Montgomery, different in many respects from any heretofore projected.*
*   The Yankee papers have frequently indicated their movements, and it would be well to be on the lookout and consider your plan of operations on the various routes of approach.*
*   Should any number of negroes cross our lines for such purpose boldness and confidence will be sure of success against any disparity of force.*
*   Maneuver to get a body of troops in their rear to cut off their retreat, and when they are routed the cavalry will pursue at a gallop, charging as foragers should they take to the woods. Those taken prisoners will be closely guarded and watched night and day by a large detail, and turned over to the State authorities as soon as practicable.*

APPENDIX

By order of Brigadier-General Walker:

JAMES LOWNDES,
Captain and Acting Assistant Adjutant-General.

These two companies (F and I) have composed for some time a portion of the command of Major Emanuel, who was absent from his command upon the occasion of my visit to his camp (to be hereafter reported). I met him in Georgetown only a few hours. It is evident that the command did not prosper under him; they have not improved as they should have done, nor are they now actively engaged in the work of improvement. Major Emanuel is not now immediately connected with them. I am informed by the officers that they drill only twice a week. They alleged as excuse heavy duties. It will be seen from this report that the duty is very light, and no reason exists why a regular and systematic daily drill, mounted and dismounted, should not be had. The companies are good companies, and only need this, under efficient officers, to take their proper position.
Respectfully submitted,

JNO. F. LAY,
Adjutant and Inspector General.

STATEMENT OF WILLIAM C. HEYWARD
IN REGARD TO THE COMBAHEE RAID

On Tuesday, June 2, 1863, at 6:15 a.m., servant knocked at door, stating that the driver, who was with the hands at work in lower fields, sent up word that there were three Yankee boats coming up the river. Immediately got up and sent word to him to bring up the hands and take them back into the woods. On first going out could not see the boats in consequence of a bend in the river. Took my glass, and on going about 100 yards from house saw a large ferry-boat, with United States flag flying, upper deck crowded with people. She came up very slowly; sent a small boat ashore; 7 men landed; walked to and from causeway blowing a horn and waving a small flag. After standing and watching boat and their proceedings for some time, say fifteen or twenty minutes, the driver came up with the hands; again gave the order to him, "Take the hands back into the woods." Asked driver if any of the pickets had passed up causeway to report; he replied, "No one has passed up since I went down to work this morning." Examined with glass carefully picket station at ferry; saw the horses standing quietly hitched. Yankee boat at that time within 1¼ miles of them. One of my hands then said, "Here they come." On my asking, "Who?" he replied, "The pickets." On again looking down causeway saw 4 men coming up, one much ahead running his horse; two shots were fired at them from boat. He came up to me and reported, "Yankee boats in river." Told him that fact was known by me at least one hour since. Asked why they were so slow in reporting. He said, "Ordered not to report until we are certain of facts; thought perhaps they might be our boats." Asked if he was the first to start to give information; he said, "Yes." Asked if any one had gone to Pocotaligo, he said, "No." Told him to hurry on to Green Pond for troops. During this time boat kept coming up, but very slowly; it was about three-fourths flood; she passed safely the point where the torpedoes were placed, and finally reached the bridge at the ferry, which they immediately commenced cutting away; landed, to all appearance, a small force at Mr. Middleton's, and in a few minutes his buildings were in flames. On again examining causeway carefully saw a body of men advancing in regular order, double-file; watched them closely and counted ten files, or 20 men; did not observe that they were negroes; waited until they were within 400 or 500 yards of gate, and no help coming, took horse and left for Green Pond. About 3 miles from plantation met 9 men on horseback, advancing slowly; told them the state of things. Officer commanding said he wished the company was with him. Observing the company coming on about one-half mile off, told him of it; went on and, meeting the company, told officer commanding the state of affairs below; heard him give the order to trot or gallop. Then went on to Green Pond and telegraphed to General Walker; whilst doing so the artillery company passed station on their way down. In a very few minutes two pieces of artillery returned; officer asked the road to Salkehatchie Bridge; told him it was 14 or 15 miles distant, and that General Walker was only 5 or 6 miles from it; said he was ordered to go there, and started. Returned to plantation as fast as possible and found, as expected, that the troops had been too late in getting down, the buildings being in flames and the negroes gone or going off the causeway and bridge when they arrived. On my return the boat was about one-half mile below the bridge; do not think she ever passed up beyond it. My negroes who were left report that the party coming up causeway divided, part going off to burn the mill, the rest coming on up to dwelling house; they also state that there was but one white man, all the rest negroes. They burnt every building on plantation except the negro quarters.

WM. C. HEYWARD.

THE *CHARLESTON MERCURY* NEWSPAPER ACCOUNT WRITTEN BY PLANTER JOSHUA NICHOLS

June 19, 1863, The Charleston Mercury
(FOR THE MERCURY.)

At 5 o'clock, a.m., June 21, 1863, I was awakened in my bed by the driver, who rushed precipitately in my room, and informed me that two of the enemy's steamers were in full sight, and would soon be opposite to my landing. I arose hastily, dressed myself with all possible speed, went upon the portico of the house, which commands an extensive view of the river and all the neighboring plantations, and, sure enough, there were the two steamers—one quite small, and the other very large, crowded with armed men in dark uniform. It seemed to me that I also saw women seated in chairs upon the upper deck of the large steamer, surveying with curiosity the beautiful and peaceful scene that lay stretched before them. It was a very pleasant morning—the sky was clear, and from the state of the atmosphere, every residence, building and mill loomed out, and seemed nearer than they really were. The rice crops were growing luxuriantly, and the negro settlements upon the hills looked like a succession of tranquil villages. The steamers did not fire a gun, and had I not known them to be the enemy by their flags, I would have supposed them a large party on a pleasure excursion. Upon perceiving that the smaller steamer was steering for my landing, I ordered the driver to bring the people to me, as they had come from the fields and were gathering at the settlement. My house servants all stood around me, professing the utmost attachment and their perfect willingness to obey my commands, but not exhibiting the slightest degree of alarm or surprise. Finding that the negros did not come to me from the settlement, as I had ordered, I immediately went there, found them all about their houses, and seeing that the enemy had now landed about twenty negros under the leadership of one white man, I ordered them to follow me and take to the woods, which form a deep forest near my house. They all professed a willingness to do so, but not one made a sign of moving. As I had not a single arm of defence about my person, I was forced to fly to the woods for protection. There is a forest which extends from my house to Mr. Kirkland's place, skirting the rice fields the whole way. I took refuge in it, and determined to watch, as far as I could, the operations of the enemy. They came up to my house, and in a very short time it was set on fire. I looked towards Mr. Kirkland's place, and soon perceived the smoke rising from the direction of his residence. Presently the mill, overseer house and stables on his place, also the threshing mill and barns upon my own place, as well as those upon Mr. Lowndes and Col. Heyward, were burning almost simultaneously. The negros, men and women, were rushing to the boat with their children, now and then greeting someone whom they recognized among the uniformed negros, and who were probably former runaways from the various plantations in the neighborhood. The negros seemed to be utterly transformed, drunk with excitement, and capable of the wildest excesses. The roaring of the flames, the barbarous howls of the negros, the blowing of horns, the harsh steam whistle, and the towering columns of smoke from every quarter, made an impression on my mind which can never be effaced. Here, I thought to myself, is a repetition of San Domingo. Remaining about five hours in the woods, I concluded to steal towards my own burning house, and ascertain the amount of destruction. I approached cautiously, as the small steamboat had not yet left my landing, and I could still see the negros carrying from my burning barn bags of rice upon their heads, in rapid movement towards the steamboat. At eleven o'clock the steamer moved off, not having left her station for six hours, and I was left alone to survey with tearful eyes the wide scene of desolation around me. My pleasant and comfortable house was in ashes. My library, containing over 3500 volumes, in the collection of which I had employed twenty years of my life; shelved thoughts of the richest minds of ancient and modern times, which I had treasured up as a consolation for the present, and as a refuge against disease and old age; every memorial I possessed of my past life, and every material object to which my heart still clung, not for its intrinsic value, but for the unspeakable associations connected with it—vanished, perished in the flames; and this was not done in a tempest, by the lightning of heaven, but sanctioned by the order of the civilized, philanthropic, liberty-loving Yankee. Besides my house, they burnt three negro houses, one of which the driver lived in, my steam threshing mill and barn, corn house, kitchen, wash kitchen and store room, mule stable, and six thousand bushels of rice. They also carried off 73 negros and three mules. What contributed most to my mortification was, that in my whole gang of slaves, among whom there were any amount of Aarons, Abrahams, Isaacs and Jacobs, there was not one Abdiel—not one remained loyal to the rebel. They left an old woman who had been bedridden for a year, and whose house was next to the driver's house that had been burnt. I went into her house and found her naked in her bed, stript [sic] of her clothing, abandoned by her children and grandchildren. She has since died. This is an instance of Abolition humanity. They all left me, saints and sinners, and nothing remains to testify of their former presence but the famishing cats and dogs, who, in coming around me, seem to demand by their *anxious expression the sense and meaning of their present loneliness. The negros were not allowed by their sympathizing friends to carry off any of their clothing, except what they wore on their backs; not a pot, nor a kettle; and there was left at the landing a strange medley of clothes, pots and kettles, baskets, bolts of cloth, hats and shoes, together with the familiar faces of many articles which had miraculously disappeared from the premises years ago, and of whose mysterious disappearance no intelligible explanation had ever been given. There was enough [illegible] to fill ten wagons. They have all gone, and I expect by this time realize the meaning of that other abstraction, liberty and the rights of man. I think old Pompey will miss his garden and his favorite vegetables; old Janus will no longer captivate his admiring audience by misquotations from the Bible; and old driver George will find his occupation gone. No ready compliance now with his commands, and no secret services rendered to his personal convenience, of which I was kept in ignorance. I have no doubt, if ever I should see that infidum again, I shall find them a wiser and sadder people. The boon of liberty they will discover, to their cost, does not comprise clothing, comfortable houses, kind treatment and medical attendance, but to them is misery, privation, hunger and a cheerless death. The question now is, could this raid have been prevented? I think so. Had Jeffords' squadron been stationed here, I think, though I profess to be no judge in military matters, the enemy could have been intercepted. They had been posted here for eighteen months, knew every foot and by-path of the country, all the plantations, and by a proper disposal of a few men upon each place, might have checked their progress. The squadron under the command of Major Manuel had been recently transferred to this country, which they did not know, from a country with which they were perfectly familiar. They were entirely ignorant of the localities, and though no doubt willing to render assistance, were unable to do so, from their want of familiarity with this region. One or two cannon at Tar Bluff, I feel confident, would have arrested the progress of the steamboats; and had the fort at Combahee Ferry retained the cannon which now repose at Green Pond, it might have done them some damage. But in these matters I say I am no judge, and these are my small opinions, besides I am in no mood for impartial criticism. It is merely my desire to give a simple and succinct account of what I saw and suffered; and, to use the language of Pius Aeneas,* quorum pars magna fui. The world should know that the valiant Yankee, despairing of conquering the Confederates in a fair field, has resorted to the easy and expeditious method of making war upon private dwellings, burning provisions, barns and store houses, and seeking to wreak his petty malice on localities where he is confident of meeting no resistance.*

This is an act commanded and sanctioned by the best of all possible governments; yes, best indeed, in the estimation of the innumerable Rev. Dr. Panglosses' that swarm over the North. To talk of reconstruction is about as sensible as to attempt the reconstruction of the Tower of Babel, or the rebuilding of the Temple of Jerusalem. They have laid me under obligations which I hope my brave countrymen will repay with interest.

FINIS.

June 19, 1863
The Charleston Mercury
The Raid on Combahee

We publish this morning a letter from an intelligent planter to a friend, descriptive of what passed under his own eye, during the late raid on the Combahee River. The matter, as presented, is one demanding the serious and careful attention of all citizens of the State, no less than the Governor, and the military authorities of this Department. The picture drawn is startling, and although painted in plain, unvarnished terms, present facts of a very grave nature and import. Viewed from several points of view, they require a deliberate and unshrinking consideration. It shall receive it at our hands—let others do their duty.

Viewed as an example permitted to others, it is most pernicious, and may be destructive in its future effects.

As a question of food, it is of moment, threatening as it does the whole grainery of the State, which lies upon the coast—for the interior of the State has produced but little more than it consumes. Lay waste, or abandon the coast, and the whole rice crop—upon which crop our armies here subsist to a very great extent—is destroyed—all fodder is destroyed for the cavalry—and the next season will find the State, as well as the army here, pinched for mere subsistence. Transportation, too, will not relieve matters. Planters cannot jeopardize their all, without some ostensible pretension towards protection.

Regarding the matter as touching international law, between ourselves and the Government of the United States, and as bearing upon the customs of war, the facts are such that they must be faced by our authorities, State and military. The course pursued by the enemy is subversive of every custom of war since the time of the Crusades, and is in violation of every law which governs the conduct of nations towards each other. As touching the laws of South Carolina, whether considered as mere slaves or as individuals domiciled here, every soul engaged in the late raid, whether white or black, has forfeited his life, either as an insurrectionist or a traitor to the State of South Carolina; and whether taken now or at any future time, the lives of these men are forfeit—and the forfeit must be paid to the last farthing, without consideration to individuals, to property, or to qualms of the stomach or of the pocket. No prisoners should be taken at all. There is a time for all things—a time to make money, and a time to spend it—a time, for sentiment, and a time for sternness. The time for the exercise of the latter sentiment has come—the time for the former folly has passed. The security of our homes and the integrity of our institutions are at stake. The violation of the laws and customs of all civilized nations is gross, palpable and indisputable. And great is the crime of foreign officers, who, in violation of all of our internal laws, seek to uproot our whole social system in anarchy—not by means of their armies or of subjugation in fair warfare, but by the foulest tools—lawlessness of the assassin and the thief. Let the adder be crushed in its incipiency, be the immediate results what they may.

Regarding the matter from a military point of view, the facts are such that they require explanation. It is stated that two steamers ran up the Combahee River in broad daylight in the morning, and come to anchor at the several landings on the river belonging to the adjoining plantations. Nothing goes to show that the steamers were even armed with a single cannon, and all the houses and settlements were on the highland, from one to two miles from the river. There they remained, undisturbed, for six mortal hours, while small bands of negroes, with one or two white men heading each, wander about and lay waste and destroy the surrounding plantations with fire and pillage. During all this time forces, said to be more than ample not only for the protection of the whole band of outlaws, fail even to interrupt this pleasant pastime of the enemy. Not an outlaw is captured or killed, and not a negro or a house saved on our part. And this has happened in a country affording, in the very highest degree, every facility for an easy defense. If all the facts stated—and they are stated on very unexceptionable authority—be true, the whole thing is most disgraceful.

The matter calls for a vigorous and a rigorous investigation. It is understood that such investigation is now being made.

The conduct of affairs at Bluffton seems to redeem the reputation of the division but little.

NOTES

*T*he *War of the Rebellion: A Compilation of the Official Records of the Union and Confederate Armies* is abbreviated as *ORA*. "Charles P. Wood manuscript" denotes the application and additional documents supporting a pension for the services of Harriet Tubman during the war. "Apthorp manuscript" is a document of the war experiences of William Apthorp, a captain in the Second South Carolina Volunteers.

Chapter 1

1. Larson, *Promised Land*, 8; Sernett, *Harriet Tubman*, 40, 46.
2. Larson, *Promised Land*, 16; Sernett, *Harriet Tubman*, 15.
3. Larson, *Promised Land*, 16–17.
4. Ibid., 15.
5. Ibid., 32–34.
6. Ibid., 37.
7. Ibid., 37–38; Bradford, *Moses of Her People*, 109.
8. Larson, *Promised Land*, 39.
9. Ibid., 40.
10. Ibid., 42; Sernett, *Harriet Tubman*, 16; Bradford, *Moses of Her People*, 109.
11. Sernett, *Harriet Tubman*, 17; Larson, *Promised Land*, 58; Bradford, *Moses of Her People*, 110.
12. Sernett, *Harriet Tubman* 17.
13. Larson, *Promised Land*, 64.

14. Ibid., 65–66.
15. Sennett, *Harriet Tubman*, 19; Larson, *Promised Land*, 73.
16. Larson, *Promised Land*, 75.
17. Ibid., 78; Bradford, *Moses of Her People*, 111.
18. Sernett, *Harriet Tubman* 21.
19. Bradford, *Moses of Her People*, 112; Larson, *Promised Land*, 89-90; Sernett, *Harriet Tubman*, 56.
20. Clinton, *Road to Freedom*, 82; Bradford, *Moses of Her People*, 112; Larson, *Promised Land*, 90.
21. Clinton, *Road to Freedom*, 83.
22. Larson, *Promised Land*, 91-92.
23. Clinton, *Road to Freedom*, 84; Larson, *Promised Land*, 92, 95.
24. Larson, *Promised Land*, 99; Clinton, *Road to Freedom*, 105, 110–12.
25. Larson, *Promised Land*, 114–18.
26. Ibid., 120–21, 124, 144, 149; Bradford, *Moses of Her People*, 115–16.
27. Larson, *Promised Land*, 63; Sernett, *Harriet Tubman*, 56, 62.
28. Sernett, *Harriet Tubman*, 78.
29. *Auburn Citizen*, March 11, 1913.
30. Bradford, *Moses of Her People*, 117.
31. Sernett, *Harriet Tubman*, 79; Larson, *Promised Land*, 350, note 9.
32. Larson, *Promised Land*, 159; Clinton, *Road to Freedom*, 129; Sernett, *Harriet Tubman*, 79.
33. Sernett, *Harriet Tubman*, 79; Larson, *Promised Land*, 161.
34. Larson, *Promised Land*, 161–62.
35. Ibid., 163–65.
36. Ibid., 166.
37. Yoseloff, *Battles and Leaders* 1.
38. Bradford, *Moses of Her People*, 93; Sernett, *Harriet Tubman*, 86; Charles P. Wood manuscript.
39. Larson, *Promised Land*, 205, 208.
40. Ibid., 204.
41. Charles P. Wood manuscript.
42. Bradford, *Moses of Her People*, 97.
43. Ibid., 98.
44. Ibid.
45. Charles P. Wood manuscript; Joshua Nichols account of the raid in the *Charleston Mercury*; William Heyward reported fifteen slaves missing shortly before the raid.
46. Looby, *Thomas Wentworth Higginson*, 251.
47. Sernett, *Harriet Tubman*, 87.

Chapter 2

48. Cutler, *History of Kansas*, 81, 83.
49. Greeley, *American Conflict* 1: 235.
50. Cutler, *History of Kansas*, 82.
51. Ibid., 83, 85, 90–91, 128.
52. Ibid., 89, 93–95.
53. Ibid., 97, 104.
54. Ibid., 124–25.
55. Ibid., 107.
56. Ibid., 130–31.
57. Ibid.
58. Ibid., 131.
59. Ibid., 302.
60. Ibid.
61. Ibid; "Commission of James Montgomery," Kansas State Historical Society.
62. Cutler, *History of Kansas*, 302; Dirck, *Hand of God*, 100–15.
63. Posse receipt seeking arrest of James Montgomery.
64. James Montgomery to George L. Sterns, October 6, 1860, George Stearns Collection, Kansas Historical Society #507. Stearns was a supporter and financial backer of Montgomery, enabling him to purchase arms and ammunition.
65. Transactions of the Kansas State Historical Society, 1900–1902 7: 28.
66. Cutler, *History of Kansas*, 43; Dirck, *Hand of God*, 107, 110, 113.
67. "Colonel James Montgomery Appointment," Kansas State Historical Society; Cutler, *History of Kansas*, 302.
68. Phillips, *Civil War on the Western Border*.
69. *ORA* Series III, Vol. III, 14; Wise, *Gate of Hell*, 48–51.

Chapter 3

70. Miller, *Lincoln's Abolitionist General*, 3, 52.
71. Ibid., 5–7.
72. Ibid., 7.
73. Ibid., 10.
74. Hunter, *Military Services of Gen. David Hunter*, 6.
75. Miller, *Lincoln's Abolitionist General*, 31–32.
76. Ibid., 33–34.
77. Ibid., 34, 37.
78. Ibid., 45–47.

79. Hunter, *Military Services of Gen. David Hunter*; David Hunter to Abraham Lincoln, October 1860, Abraham Lincoln Papers, Library of Congress.

80. Hunter, *Military Services of Gen. David Hunter*, 8.

81. Ibid., 8; Miller, *Lincoln's Abolitionist General*, 56.

82. Hunter, *Military Services of Gen. David Hunter*, 8; Miller, *Lincoln's Abolitionist General*, 58.

83. Miller, *Lincoln's Abolitionist General*, 69; Hunter, *Military Services of Gen. David Hunter*, 9.

84. Hunter, *Military Services of Gen. David Hunter*, 9–10, 12.

85. Miller, *Lincoln's Abolitionist General*, 76.

86. Ibid., 89–91.

87. Ibid., 78.

88. Ibid., 82–85.

89. Lincoln letter, Abraham Lincoln Papers, Library of Congress.

90. Hunter letter, Abraham Lincoln Papers, Library of Congress.

91. Miller, *Lincoln's Abolitionist General*, 79.

92. Ibid., 87.

Chapter 4

93. *ORA* Series I, Vol. VI, 248.

94. Hunter, *Military Services of Gen. David Hunter, 16.*

95. Wise, Smith and Grigg, *Charleston to Savannah Railroad Defenses*; Miller, *Lincoln's Abolitionist General*, 94–95.

96. Miller, *Lincoln's Abolitionist General*, 95.

97. Ibid; Elmore, *Hunter's Proclamation*, 23.

98. Miller, *Lincoln's Abolitionist General*, 95; Pearson, *Letters from Port Royal*, 2.

99. Miller, *Lincoln's Abolitionist General*, 98; *ORA* Series I, Vol VI, 133–34.

100. *ORA* Series I, Vol. XIV, 341.

101. Miller, *Lincoln's Abolitionist General*, 97; *ORA* Series I, Vol. 14, 337; Pearson, *Letters from Port Royal*, 133.

102. Pearson, *Letters from Port Royal*, 341.

103. Wise, *Gate of Hell*, 45.

104. Abraham Lincoln Papers, Library of Congress, Series 1, General Correspondence, 1833–1916.

105. *ORA* Series I, Vol. VI, 176.

106. Miller, *Lincoln's Abolitionist General*, 105.

107. Pearson, *Letters from Port Royal*, 48.

108. Ash, *Firebrand of Liberty*, 35; Pearson, *Letters from Port Royal*, 40.

109. Pearson, *Letters from Port Royal*, 39–40.

110. Ibid., 40.
111. Miller, *Lincoln's Abolitionist General*, 104.
112. Ibid., 105.
113. Hunter, *Military Services of Gen. David Hunter*, 24–25; Dobak, *Freedom by the Sword*, 32.
114. Miller, *Lincoln's Abolitionist General*, 106.
115. *ORA* Series I, Vol. XIV, 363.
116. Miller, *Lincoln's Abolitionist General*, 113.
117. *ORA* Series I, Vol. XIV, 375–77; Miller, *Lincoln's Abolitionist General*, 113, 127; Dobak, *Freedom by the Sword*, 33.
118. Miller, *Lincoln's Abolitionist General*, 129.

Chapter 5

119. Westwood, *Black Troops*, 67.
120. *ORA* Series 1, Vol. XIV, 377.
121. Looby, *Thomas Wentworth Higginson*, 13–15.
122. Ibid., 251.
123. Higginson, *Army Life in a Black Regiment*, 18, 29; Ash, *Firebrand of Liberty*, 35.
124. Higginson, *Army Life in a Black Regiment*, 30.
125. Ash, *Firebrand of Liberty*, 92–93.
126. Apthorp manuscript; Looby, *Thomas Wentworth Higginson*, 104.
127. Looby, *Thomas Wentworth Higginson*, 167, 122.
128. Pearson, *Letters from Port Royal*, 185.
129. Looby, *Wentworth Higginson*, 105.
130. *ORA* Series III, Vol. III, 424.
131. Ibid., Series I, Vol. XIV, 196.
132. Higginson, *Army Life in a Black Regiment*, 108.
133. Pearson, *Letters from Port Royal*, 185.
134. Apthorp manuscript.
135. Ibid.
136. Ibid.
137. Ibid; Higginson, *Army Life in a Black Regiment*, 120.
138. Apthorp manuscript; *ORA* Series I, Vol. XIV, 233.
139. Ibid.

Chapter 6

140. Yoseloff, *Battles and Leaders* 1: 685–86.
141. Ibid; *ORA* Series I, Vol. VI, 25.
142. Wise, *Gate of Hell*, 10.
143. *ORA* Series I, Vol. VI, 25.
144. *Mapping the Charleston to Savannah Railroad Defenses* 15 - 15.
145. de la Cova, Cuban Confederate Colonel 162.
146. *Mapping the Charleston to Savannah Railroad Defenses* 16.
147. Ibid.
148. Ibid., 14–18.
149. *Letters of Samuel McKittrick*, Kennesaw Mountain Battlefield Park. Accessed through Batsonm.tripod.com/letters/letters29a.html.
150. Wise, Smith and Grigg, *Charleston to Savannah Railroad Defenses*, 118.
151. Ibid.
152. Ibid., 73–107.
153. Emilio, *Brave Black Regiment*, 278.
154. Rowland, *History of Beaufort County*, 122.
155. Wise, Smith and Grigg, *Charleston to Savannah Railroad Defenses*, 82.
156. Ibid., 87, 90.
157. Map by Major Orlando Poe, Chief Engineer, Union, Library of Congress.
158. Wise, Smith and Grigg, Charleston *to Savannah Railroad Defenses*, 95.
159. Ibid 59.

Chapter 7

160. *ORA* Series I, Vol. XIV, 307.
161. Ibid., 190.
162. Ibid., 930.
163. Ibid., 291.
164. Ibid., 945–46.
165. Ibid., 945.
166. Ibid., 946.
167. Ibid., 307.
168. Ibid., 292. (See Special Order No. 112.)
169. Ibid., 293.
170. Higginson, *Army Life in a Black Regiment*, 80.
171. Apthorp manuscript.
172. Ibid; Denison, Shot *and Shell*, 155.

173. Charles P. Wood manuscript; Bradford, *Moses of Her People*, 99; *ORA* Series I, Vol. XIV, 195.

174. Apthorp manuscript.

175. Mahan, *Treatise on Field Fortifications*.

176. *ORA* Series I, Vol. XIV, 290–308.

177. Apthorp manuscript.

178. Ibid.

179. *Harper's Weekly*, July 4, 1863.

180. Apthorp manuscript.

181. Bradford, *Moses of Her People*, 100–01.

182. *ORA* Series I, Vol. XIV, 290–308.

183. Ibid.

184. Denison, *Shot and Shell*, 156.

185. *ORA* Series I, Vol. XIV, 301.

186. Denison, *Shot and Shell*, 156.

187. Ibid.

188. *ORA* Series I, Vol. XIV, 307–08.

189. Ibid., 290–308.

190. Ibid.

191. Ibid.

192. Ibid.

193. Apthorp manuscript; *ORA* Series I Vol. XIV 290–308.

194. *ORA* Series I, Vol. XIV, 301.

195. Ibid., 302.

196. Ibid., 303.

197. Ibid.

198. Ibid., 304.

199. Apthorp manuscript.

200. Ibid.

201. Fifth South Carolina Cavalry Regimental History.

202. *ORA* Series I, Vol. XIV, 463; Bradford, *Scenes in the Life of Harriet Tubman*, 86.

Chapter 8

203. *ORA* Series I, Vol. XIV, 463.

204. *New South*, June 6, 1863.

205. *Harper's Weekly*, July 4, 1863.

206. *Wisconsin State Journal*, June 20, 1863.

207. Sernett, *Harriet Tubman*, 92.

208. *ORA* Series I, Vol. XIV, 291.
209. Journal of Meta Morris Grimball.
210. Hollis, *South Carolina Rice Fields*, 29–30.
211. ORA Series I, Vol. XIV, 298–306.
212. Freemantle, *Three Months in the Southern States*, 66, 73.
213. *Charleston Mercury*, June 19, 1863.
214. Looby, *Thomas Wentworth Higginson*, 158.
215. Ibid., 288.
216. *ORA* Series I, Vol. XIV, 462; Duncan, *Blue Eyed Child of Fortune*, 42, 356.
217. Duncan, *Blue Eyed Child of Fortune*, 339.
218. *ORA* Series I, Vol. XIV, 466.
219. Ibid., Vol. XXVIII, 11–12.

Chapter 9

220. Sernett, *Harriet Tubman*, 91.
221. Milton Sennett personal comm.
222. Senrett, *Harriet Tubman*, 90; www.smithsonianmag.com/history/harriet-tubmans-amazing-grace-53824293/.
223. Allen, *Intelligence in the Civil War*.
224. Apthorp manuscript.
225. *ORA* Series I, Vol. XIV, 463.
226. Bradford, *Moses of Her People*, 99.
227. Bradford, *Scenes in the Life of Harriet Tubman*, 71; Charles P. Wood manuscript; *Congressional Globe*, Plowden pension.
228. *Wisconsin State Journal*, June 20, 1863.
229. Porcher, Harriet Tubman analysis.
230. Bradford, *Moses of Her People*, 103.
231. *ORA* Series I, Vol. VI, 91.
232. Sernett, *Harriet Tubman*, 92.
233. Larson, *Promised Land*, 222.
234. www.harriettubmanbiography.com/harriet-tubman-myths-and-facts.html.

BIBLIOGRAPHY

The Abraham Lincoln Papers at the Library of Congress, Series 1. General Correspondence, 1833–1916. Transcribed and annotated by the Lincoln Studies Center, Knox College, Galesburg, Illinois.

Allen, Thomas. *Intelligence in the Civil War*. Washington, D.C.: Central Intelligence Agency, 2007.

Apthorp, William L. "Montgomery's Raids in Florida, Georgia, and South Carolina." Apthorp Family Papers, 1741–1964. Historical Museum of Southern Florida.

Ash, Stephen V. *Firebrand of Liberty*. New York: W.W. Norton & Company, 2008.

Auburn Citizen. March 11, 1913.

Bradford, Sarah. *Harriet Tubman: The Moses of Her People*. 1886. Reprint, New York: Citadel Press, 1989.

———. *Scenes in the Life of Harriet Tubman*. N.p.: Dennis Brothers & Company, 1869.

Burton, E. Milby. *The Siege of Charleston, 1861–1865*. Columbia: University of South Carolina Press, 1970.

Castel, Albert. "Kansas Jayhawking Raids into Western Missouri in 1861." *Missouri Historical Review* 54, no. 1 (October 1959).

Charleston Mercury. June 19, 1863; July 3, 1863; May 28, 1862.

Clinton, Catherine. *Harriet Tubman*. New York: Little, Brown & Company, 2004.

Congressional Globe. February 24, 1869. (Bill H.R. No. 1323 for the relief of Walter Plowden.)

Cutler, William G. *History of the State of Kansas*. Chicago: A.T. Andreas, 1883.

de la Cova, Antonio Rafael. *Cuban Confederate Colonel: The Life of Ambrosio Jose Gonzales*. Columbia: University of South Carolina Press, 2003.

———. The Family Papers of Ambrosio Jose Gonzales. Letters, documents and articles compiled by Antonio de la Cova. January 2000.

Denison, Frederic Reverend. *Shot and Shell: The Third Rhode Island Heavy Artillery Regiment in the Rebellion, 1861–1864*. Providence, RI: J.A. & R.A. Reid, 1879.

Dirck, Brian R. "By the Hand of God: James Montgomery and Redemptive Violence." *Kansas History* 27 (Spring–Summer 2004): 100–15.

Dobak, William A. *Freedom by the Sword*. Washington, D.C.: U.S. Army Center of Military History, 2011.

Duncan, Russell, ed. *Blue-Eyed Child of Fortune: The Civil War Letters of Colonel Robert Gould Shaw*. Athens: University of Georgia Press, 1992.

Dyer, Fredrick. *A Compendium of the War of the Rebellion*. Vols. 1–5. New York: Thomas Yoseloff, 1959.

Elmore, Charles J., PhD. *General David Hunter's Proclamation*. Fort Washington, PA: Eastern National, 2002

Emilio, Luis F. *A Brave Black Regiment: The History of the Fifty-Fourth Regiment of Massachusetts Volunteer Infantry, 1863–1865*. 1894. Reprint, Cambridge, MA: Da Capo Press, 1995.

Freemantle, Lieutenant Colonel. *Three Months in the Southern States: April–June 1863*. New York: J. Bradburn, 1864.

Goodrich, Thomas. *Black Flag: Guerrilla Warfare on the Western Border, 1861–1865*. Bloomington: Indiana University Press, 1999

Greeley, Horace. *The American Conflict*. 2 vols. Hartford, CT: O.D. Case & Company, 1867.

Grimball, Meta Morris. *Journal of Meta Morris Grimball*. Transcribed by Cynthia Porcher, Wilson Library, University of North Carolina, Chapel Hill.

Higginson, Thomas Wentworth. *Army Life in a Black Regiment*. 1869. Reprint, New York: W.W. Norton and Company, 1984.

Hollis, Margaret Belser, and Allen H. Stokes, eds. *Twilight on the South Carolina Rice Fields*. Columbia: University of South Carolina Press, 2010.

Hunter, David. *Report of the Military Services of Gen. David Hunter, U.S.A., During the War of the Rebellion Made to the U.S. War Department*. 2nd ed. New York: D. Van Nostrand Co., 1892.

Kansas State Historical Society. *Transactions of the Kansas State Historical Society, 1901–1902*. Vol. 7. Topeka: Kansas State Historical Society, 1902.

Larson, Kate Clifford. *Bound for the Promised Land: Harriet Tubman: Portrait of an American Hero*. New York: Ballentine Books, 2004.

Linder, Suzanne Cameron. *Historical Atlas of the Rice Plantations of the ACE River Basin, 1860*. Columbia: South Carolina Department of Archives and History, 1995.

Looby, Christopher, ed. *The Complete Civil War Journal and Selected Letters of Thomas Wentworth Higginson*. Chicago: University of Chicago Press, 2000.

Mahan, Dennis H. *A Treatise on Field Fortifications*. 3rd edition. New York: John Wiley and Sons, 1861.

Miller, Edward A. *Lincoln's Abolitionist General*. Columbia: University of South Carolina Press, 1997.

Montgomery, James. Letter to George L. Sterns, October 6, 1860. George Stearns Collection, Kansas Historical Society.

The New South. June 6, 1863.

Pearson, Elizabeth Ware, ed. *Letters from Port Royal*. Boston: W.B. Clarke Company, 1906,

Phillips, Christopher. "Montgomery, James." Civil War on the Western Border. http://www.civilwaronthewesternborder.org/content/montgomery-james.

Rowland, Lawrence, Alexander Moore and George C. Rogers. *The History of Beaufort County, South Carolina: 1514–1861*. Columbia: University of South Carolina Press, 1996.

Schafer, Daniel L. *Thunder on the River: The Civil War in Northeast Florida*. Gainesville: University Press of Florida, 2010.

Sernett, Milton C. *Harriet Tubman: Myth, Memory and History*. Durham, NC: Duke University Press, 2007.

Smith, D.E. Huger. *A Charlestonian's* Recollections, 1846–1913. Charleston, SC: Carolina Art Association, 1950.

Smith, Steven, Stephen R. Wise and Jeff W. Grigg. *Mapping the Charleston to Savannah Railroad Defenses: Phase II*. South Carolina Institute of Archaeology and Anthropology, 2011.

Stone, H. David, Jr. *Vital Rails: The Charleston & Savannah Railroad and the Civil War in Coastal South Carolina*. Columbia: University of South Carolina Press, 2008.

Taylor, Susie King. *A Black Woman's Civil War Memoirs*. Edited by Patricia W. Romero. 1902. Reprint, Princeton, NJ: Markus Wiener Publishing, 1988.

United States Congress. *Report of the Special Committee Appointed to Investigate the Troubles in Kansas*. Washington, D.C.: C. Wendell, printer, 1856.

United States Department of War. *Map of the Rebel Lines of the Pocotaligo, Combahee & Ashepoo [Rivers], South Carolina*. Washington, D.C.: United States Department of War, 1866.

The War of the Rebellion: A Compilation of the Official Records of the Union and Confederate Armies. Washington, D.C.: U.S. Government Printing Office, 1882.

Westwood, Howard C. *Black Troops, White Commanders and Freedmen During the Civil War*. Southern Illinois University Press, 2008.

———. "Generals David Hunter and Rufus Saxton and Black Soldiers." *South Carolina Historical Magazine* 86, no. 3 (July 1985): 165–81.

Williams, George W. *A History of the Negro Troops in the War of the Rebellion.* New York: Harper & Brothers, 1888.

Wilson, Joseph T. *The Black Phalanx.* 1887. Reprint, Cambridge, MA: Da Capo Press, 1994.

Wisconsin State Journal. June 20, 1863.

Wise, Stephen R. *Gate of Hell: Campaign for Charleston, 1863.* Columbia: University of South Carolina Press, 1994.

Yoseloff, Thomas. *Battles and Leaders of the Civil War.* 4 vols. New York: Thomas Yoseloff, Inc., 1956.

INDEX

ABOUT THE AUTHOR

J eff W. Grigg is a resident of Green Pond, South Carolina, located just a few miles from Combahee Ferry. He is a member of the Civil War Fortification Study Group, a group dedicated to the preservation and interpretation of Civil War earthen fortifications. He has served on the board of directors and as vice-president of the Colleton Country Historical and Preservation Society. He also served on the board of directors of the South Carolina Battleground Trust. Under the auspices of the South Carolina Institute of Archaeology and Anthropology, Grigg coauthored *Mapping the Charleston and Savannah Railroad Defenses: Phase II*, made possible by a grant from the American Battlefield Protection Program of the National Park Service. He was a presenter on the history of the Combahee Ferry at the dedication of the Harriet Tubman Bridge in 2008.